ON THE EDGE OF WAR

By

George C. Larsen

TO:
Eddie & Shirley

George C Larsen
a Pearl Harbor Survivor !

This book is a work of non-fiction. Names and places have been changed to protect the privacy of all individuals. The events and situations are true.

ISBN: 1-4107-8561-0 (e-book)
ISBN: 1-4107-8560-2 (Paperback)

Library of Congress Control Number: 2003095908

This book is printed on acid free paper.

Printed in the United States of America
Bloomington, IN

1stBooks – rev. 09/25/03

Chapter 1.

The Beginning!

The U.S. Coast Guard was part of the Treasury Department. In 1939 they took over the Light House systems, aids to navigation, inland water navigation systems and phased out most of the civil service personnel who wished to leave or retire that year.

That same year I had been unemployed most of the time, except for a few hours a month working at the local distillery's bottling plant in Sausalito, California. I lived with my folks in the little town of

Mill Valley, just a stone's throw from the distillery. That same year, Adolph Hitler started World War Two! This was also the year that I became aware of a movement called the Draft, it had not become a reality yet but the way things were going in Europe it sure looked like a possibility. So with that hanging over me, I decided to beat the draft by joining the Navy or the Coast Guard. Several friends of mine had joined the Navy, so I checked it out and found that they had to sign up for a six-year enlistment. Then I saw a short news reel at the local theater about the Coast Guard. Upon investigating I found out that they had a three-year enlistment, which sounded much better than the Navy enlistment. So I hustled over to the Customs House on Samson street, in San Francisco, where I was interviewed by a recruiting officer, at least I thought he was an officer, because he had five gold stripes on his left sleeve. Later on, after I passed both the physical and mental test, I found out he was a grizzly ole Chief Boatswain mate with more than twenty years of service and the gold stripes meant he had never been court marshaled, in other words he had twenty years of good conduct. It was October 29, 1939 when I took the oath. After going home to gather toiletries and change of clothes, I prepared to go to boot camp. The next day I went back to Samsone street to get my orders and home to say good bye to my folks. I returned to the Custom's House for my travel orders and found out that I would be in charge of two other recruits until we got to the training station which was located in Port Townsend, Washington. We took the ferry over to Oakland, California and boarded the train for Seattle, Washington. We arrived in Seattle around 5:00 P.M. the next day. We found out that the ferry we had to take would not be leaving for Port Townsend until 10:00 P.M. that night. We walked around town and did a little seeing. Seattle looked like a miniature San Francisco to me. They even had a short cable car system. We finally boarded the Black Ball Ferry for Port Townsend around 9:45 P.M. and arrived there around 2:00 A.M. We walked off the ship and looked around for an escort or representative to take us to the training station. After a few minutes on the sidewalk outside of the ferry building we realized that there was no one to greet us. I figured that we should walk to the facility. There was a policeman on the corner, so I asked him where the Coast Guard Station was and he gave me a blank look, because he didn't know of such a place. I finally found a taxi driver who said he knew of it but it was a little out of town. We decided that we should take the taxi, since we didn't know how far the training station was. After a short trip he pulled up to the Coast Guard entrance to the training station. We found out that no one expected

us and we had to find some place to lie down until ·
the place awoke at 6 A.M. At this time I began to
wonder about the good old Coast Guard. Did I
make a mistake? The morning came and the three
of us met finally someone who could check us in
and give us our uniforms and all the rest of the
goodies that we would need to carry out our training
in the Coast Guard.

After collecting all our clothes and GI shoes,
we were handed a stencil paper with our names on it
and were told to stencil all our clothes on the inside,
so that we could identify our things at all times.
That chore took most of the first day to finish.

The weather around Port Townsend was
miserable, it rained most of the time that I pulled
guard duty and the 30:06 Springfield rifle actually
had water in the barrel from the wind driven ice cold
rain. We had a few liberties in town but there
wasn't too much to do in that small community.

They did have an indoor roller rink and then there was Sunday Church. As the first group of recruits to go through this place, we had to help with setting up the station. They taught us how to row a boat, how to march, to dress, to salute and most important, to obey orders.

Our group finished the training period around December 15th and we advanced to our next pay grade, "2nd class seaman." This meant a pay raise from 21 dollars a month to the huge sum of 36 dollars. Then we were told to get ready for a transfer to Base Eleven in Alameda, California. I couldn't believe how lucky I was to be in the Bay area during Christmas. At the base some of us were put to work on the old ice breaker Northland. We chipped off rust spots and painted the chipped places over with red lead. After a week of that I was transferred to a patrol boat named the Arriadne, a 165 foot cutter. I got to spend Christmas at home with my family, but only for a couple of days. We did a lot of patrols, like trailing passenger ships into the harbor making sure they didn't try dropping contraband goods over the side for their associates in small boats to pick up later. This was just one of the many ways to bypass law officers and custom agents. We were sent down to Monterey Bay to be the official ship to lead the opening day of fishing and boating celebration. We were invited to a crab feed by the Monterey officials but to our disappointment the captain decided that we had to get back to San Francisco. On the way I was assigned to a lookout station on the starboard wing of the bridge. The sea began to get a little rough and the wind started to pick up. The captain kept our speed up and we started to get spray over the bridge. I had never experienced this type of spray before, it hit my face hard and felt like somebody was throwing gravel at me! After two hour's I got off of that watch and hit the sack. We ended our trip the next morning anchoring in San Francisco Bay just off of the Marina district.

Chapter 2.

A New Assignment.

After about three months duty on the Arriadne they transferred Scott Berryman and me to Hawaii. We both had been a little too smart around the old timers on board, so, I'm sure they were glad to see us get transferred.

We boarded the Navy transport USS Henderson. What a tub! It was an old German freighter that we confiscated during World War 1. She was converted into a transport that made the trip between San Francisco and China many times, stopping at ports like Pearl Harbor, Manila and Guam, dropping off naval personnel at each port. Her ship designation was AP1 which meant that she was the first ship assigned to transport duty for the US Navy. She was known to have the Navy's biggest cannon on board. It had an 18-inch bore, 2 inches more than any U.S. battle ship. The cannon was used for ballast and it lay in the bilges of the ship. The trip to Pearl Harbor took 8 days. We sun bathed on the boat deck every day so that when we got to the Hawaiian Islands we would have a head start on getting a good tan. While sun bathing on the boat deck, we couldn't help but notice that the ship was very limber. It was fascinating to see the mast up towards the bow twist to the right while the stern was twisting to the left!

After our arrival in Pearl Harbor we were transported to our new ship the CGC Roger B. Taney, W37. She was a beautiful 327 foot 2000 ton ship that was painted completely white. On the Taney I was assigned a bunk in the area we called the glory hole, this was deep down in the forward part of the ship! The routine on her was something like this, starting at about six in the morning you got up, dressed in dungarees and went bare-footed on deck to help scrub the teak wood decks with brooms, using salt water from the bay as the main source of cleansing, until the bosun's mate thought that the deck was clean enough eat off of it. Then we knocked off for breakfast and after that they assigned us to chores like chipping paint where there were rust spots and polishing all the brass works. There was plenty of brass including the turn buckles on the life lines, ships bell, etc. After seeing what you had to do as a seaman I decided to strike for a radio position. This isn't like a labor strike, it means I was going to study hard to become a radio operator. On my time off I went to lectures on antenna systems and electronics, given by a radio Ham (amateur) instructor, down at the YMCA in Honolulu. After about a month of routine work as a deck hand, we were sent up to the gunnery practice range for target practice. They loaded us in the back of a truck and drove us up to the Punch Bowel, a part of an old volcano, where there were rifle targets and pistol targets set up for us to use. On the rifle shoot out, I was given a brief run down on what and how to shoot with a Springfield Rifle 30.06. I must have missed some of the lecture because after firing the first shot I had a bruised thumb and a black eye or nearly so. After getting the swabby, a flag waving back and forth at the site of the target, meaning I had missed the target completely, 200 hundred yards away, I noticed that everyone else had lifted a sight upright on the back end of the barrel, while I had been just using the V sight that was just like my 22 rifle I used back home. Most of my shots up till then had gone into the under brush in front of my target and I was embarrassed. I did manage to hit the target after adjusting the elevation on my sights but I would never get a trophy for shooting a rifle. Next we had pistol firing with the famous colt 45 1911 model. This time I paid closer attention to the lecture on how to squeeze the trigger and what not to do while holding the gun, such as turning around with the gun in hand to ask some one a question. My first shot was a dandy, as I pulled on the trigger the pistol started facing a downward slant and I hit the paste pot right in the middle, to the merriment of all the shooters. It was a good thing that it was sitting just to the left of the target holder. After that I focused on holding the gun straight and squeezing the trigger until it finally fired, thus hitting the target some where near the bull's eye. I missed expert by eight points, so they told me to be ready to do the pistol shooting again in the morning because I had come so close to the required points for expert.

The next morning I tried again but missed it again by 6 points, so I made sharp shooter but that didn't give me anything but a notation in my records. As a seaman I had many different jobs, like polishing brass, standing watches, being the helmsman, doing lookout on the wing of the bridge, bow or in the crow's nest. One time I had the helm while coming in the channel to the harbor. The captain complimented me on my steering ability because I never drifted off course, when the quartermaster heard that compliment coming from ths captain he immediately relieved me from the wheel saying that it was his job to bring the ship into the harbor, I think he was afraid that I might steal his job! On one occasion the boatswain mate put Scott and me in the chain locker, our job was to chip off the rust and paint the bulk head with Norfolk red lead. Scott took the port side and I took the starboard, there was a partition between the anchor chains, with foot holes built in it so that we could climb around or out of the chain locker. The first thing I noticed was Scott's shoes sticking through the step holes. So, without any hesitation I lightly brushed my paint brush across his toes without him detecting my devious work! About that time the boatswain mate stuck his head into the hatch and ordered us to secure the job because we were going to sea on a rescue mission. We climbed out or the chain locker and dropped the hatch door shut and dogged it down. That is when we both noticed that our shoes were painted on the tips with Norfolk red lead. We had a big laugh over that! We found out we were going to sea to take an injured engineer from a merchant ship, as they were not coming into Honolulu and he needed medical attention! It seems that he fell into the machinery during the night and we could get him to the hospital faster than the old merchant ship. The sea was rough going out and we could see why the engineer could have slipped on the deck during this rough weather. The Taney was having a little trouble also, the chief engineer couldn't keep the ship properly balanced! The ship seemed to be heavy up by the bow, so the engineers were shifting fuel and water around trying to bring the ship balanced. After much studying and investigating, they discovered that the chain locker was full of water. This made the bow heavier than it was supposed to be and it was quite noticeable when she dove into a trough and the bow came up rather sluggishly. They found both the port and starboard port holes had been left open and this caused the locker to fill up as we dove into the heavy seas. Guess who caught it for leaving the ports open, not us, which put us on bad terms with the bosun. We picked up the injured man and returned to Honolulu the next day. Whenever we docked, we always docked bow first but this time the skipper decided to dock stern first. We were slowly easing into our berth when the captain ordered the quartermaster to ring up slow ahead on the annunciators both port and starboard screws, standing on the wing of the bridge I could see that we were moving closer and closer to the sea wall, apparently our screws were in the backward mode and the captain was yelling into the voice tube to the engine room, "I want both engines in the forward mode!" Just then the stern hit the seawall, which was about four feet of solid concrete, the ship jolted to a stop, I banged against the railing and many sailors fell as it was such an unexpected stop! The explanation on why the engine room was in reverse instead of forward, was that they always went into reverse while docking and they thought some green horn had made a mistake and rang up the annunciators wrong.

Needless to say we put a huge hole in the retaining wall, it was a good thing that no one was walking by, on the side walk, as they could have been severely injured. As soon as we were tied up securely I walked back to the stern to see what kind of damage that hard hit had caused to our stern? To my surprise the only thing I could detect was a slight indentation about the size of an egg, we marveled at the strength of that kind of a stern, which we called a cruiser stern, it came to a point instead of being a flat or rounded configuration. In the month of June we began loading huge containers full of supplies for the Line Islands, Palmyra, Canton and Enderbury. The containers were loaded by using an airplane derrick that had been put on the after deck for the seaplane that she would ordinarily would carry. They gave up on carrying the plane because it was hard to put it in the water from the ship, they had tried it and damaged the plane too much to fly. Since they now had so much extra room on the after deck, they loaded all the containers there with the use of the airplane derrick. After the loading was complete I was told that I was to be transferred to the buoy tender Kukui the next morning. I was disappointed because this meant I wouldn't make the trip to the Line Islands. I figured that it was that bosun's idea to get rid of trouble maker! As I was leaving the Taney with my seabag and mattress, the quartermaster on duty at the gangway pulled me aside and gave me a short lecture on how to make a good appearance on board the Kukui. His advice was, "what ever job they give you, work as hard as you can on it, even if you think it doesn't require that much energy. Do it, they will be watching you for about a week, after that they will probably forget all about you and then you can slack off if you want to." I thanked quartermaster Sheldon for his advice and proceeded down the gangway with my seabag and mattress. I walked over to the Kukui hoping for a good assignment there. It was only a few blocks away, it was the first pier in the harbor as you came into Honolulu. That pier was named pier Four. As I walked towards the buoy tender I wondered how I should approach them on my idea of striking for a radio position? I also thought that I should heed quartermaster Sheldon's warning about how to conduct one's self on a new ship.

Chapter 3.

The Buoy Tender

I must confess, that is exactly what I did and it worked. After about a month I asked the captain if I could try out for radioman. I got an OK from the skipper and spent the rest of my time on board the Kukui in the radio shack. I had good instruction from a second class radioman by the name of Earl Blackwood. While on the Kukui I made first class seaman and was now earning fifty four dollars a month. We still had a few lighthouse personnel on board who were working until their retirement, most of them were native Hawaiians. I got to know them well and began learning some Hawaiian phrases such as ali ma laya, which meant lower away, one of the useful expressions in working with putting a buoy into the water, which was one of the main duties for the buoy tender. One of the interesting things I learned about my fellow Hawaiian ship mates was some of their eating habits. They had a barrel of sour poi stowed away up on the bow of the ship right near the steam donkey engine, this was used to tightened the bow line with, it spun the winch machinery around and tighten the line to pull the bow of the ship towards the dock for tie up. The poi was stored in a locker next to the winch. Another goodie they had was a mason jar full of smoked salmon and rock salt. They would toss a chunk of salmon down their mouths and dip their fingers in the sour poi, pop that into their mouth and wash that down with some Japanese wine, usually saki! While we were out attending our duties changing buoys and fixing automatic lights, we sometimes anchored off shore. The Hawaiians would break out fishing line at night and fish for small fish similar to perch. They would hang a lantern out over the side to attract the fish. When they caught one they would remove a muscle from the fish's gullet that glowed from the light of the lantern and attracted the next fish more quickly. Then they gutted the fish and hung them out to dry up on the bow of the ship. After they dried they would eat them with sour poi. When ever we came to a spot were there were rocks for shell fish to hang to on the Hawaiians would harvest some. One of the shell fish was called opiis, in English it sounded like oh pea ease. It was a single sided shell fish like an abalone but was very small, about the diameter of a twenty five cent piece, you could remove the meat with the flick of your thumb. I tried all of these gourmet delights and much to my surprise I enjoyed every morsel. The Hawaiians came to like me and told me all kinds of stories about their plants, fish, birds and taboos. They told me about Niihau as we went by that Island, how it was restricted to native born Hawaiians only and about the fat cows they raised over there. They were so fat that when it rained the water couldn't roll off their backs. They described the plant called arrowroot as a powerful drug if you steamed the roots and caught the juice for drinking, it would paralyze your body to the point of having no feelings.

In our off duty time we spent a lot of time reading and sometimes we would play cards, such as poker or black jack and play for money. Other times there would be a good crap shoot down in the crews quarters. The Hawaiians loved to gamble. One night I came in from liberty and found them shooting dice in the crews quarter. I joined the group and got a hot streak and won a lot of money. In fact some of the crew started borrowing money from me so they could continue playing. At about four A.M. I decided to quit, I left with quite a bit of money and some out on loan. It was many weeks later before I got all of my money back.

The next morning when I got up I counted a very large amount of green backs, so I decided to go into town and purchase something that I always wanted, a portable radio. My friend Scott came over from the Taney and went with me to find a store that sold radio's. We found an Emerson portable, the price was right, so I bought it. We then decided that we should have an automobile to get around the Island in our days off. Believe it or not, we found an old Knute Rockne Studebaker four door sedan, with an asking price of $60:00. We offered the salesman $50:00 which he excepted. Then I needed to get a Hawaiian driver's license. The salesman said it would be better if I took his car for the test. I accepted and took his car down to the DMV office and got the license. Scott and I jumped into the old Rockne, vintage about 1930, and started out for pier Four where the Kukui was docked. I was about to make a right turn and found out the steering was faulty, it would hardly turn and I couldn't make the car negotiate the corner. We were on the street where the street cars were running and I had to back up, blocking the street car, while trying to make that simple turn. I was embarrassed and realized why that guy offered me his car for the license test. We made it to pier Four and jacked up the front end to look at the problem. We saw where the front axle had slipped along the U bolt and had the left front wheel about three inches forward of the right wheel. We worked on that and fix it by eye. The steering was normal after that so we had a car we were able to drive all around the Island. We often invited several crew members to go with us over to Makapu Pt. for body surfing and swimming.

After much practice and studying I made third class radioman. This put me in a different position or status with the crew. I was now a petty officer and my pay rate was sixty dollars a month My friend Scott and I decided to look for a small sail boat since we could now afford one as he had made coxswain and made sixty a month also. We found an ad in the newspaper for an old sailing boat, a Snipe class boat, for about fifty dollars. We drove out to the location, near Pearl Harbor, found the place where this old Snipe was and saw why the boat was for sale at fifty dollars. A Snipe is a center board type sloop and this one had a completely rotten center board box. The hull was in pretty good shape but needed a complete caulking job. We bought the Snipe from the owners, two naval

Lieutenants, who gave us the sails and the mast but no guy wire with which to rig the mast.

We tossed the hull on top of our Stude along with the mast and drove back to pier Four where we unloaded our Classic Snipe. The hull was made of mahogany and it really was an original classic snipe, though in really bad shape. We unbolted the dry rotted center board box and took it over to a small boat works where a Japanese boat builder said he could duplicate the box exactly. He did a perfect job and now we had to find a sheet of iron to put in the box for our center board keel. The boat yard people found just what we needed in a piece of one quarter inch sheet iron cut to fit our center board box. We caulked, painted and fitted the new center board box into our boat, then rigged the mast with new guy wire and turn buckles all around. With plenty of help from our friends in the crew and paint donated by Scott's skipper Chief Warrant Mazzoni,

Captain of the CGC Tiger. Scott had been transferred to the Tiger in the fall of 1940. We launched our snipe in the spring of 1941.

After checking it out in the Honolulu Harbor, we decided to try it out off shore. One young seaman asked if he could go along, we said, "sure," so he jumped in and off we sailed out the channel to the blue sea and headed up towards Kewalo Basin. The boat sure handled well. The time was around sixteen hundred and it was time to head back to the ship, as chow time was around eighteen hundred. Just as we came about a sharp gust of wind hit the our sails and a loud crack sounded as our mast snapped off at the level of the deck. We quickly grabbed all of the sails and the mast, making sure we had everything. We surveyed the damage and started figuring out how to jury rig the sails so that we could sail back to home base. After trying to set some kind of a temporary mast, to no avail, we removed the short piece of the mast that sat in the hole that went down to the keel inside the hull. Using this as a paddle we started moving towards the Honolulu Harbor channel entrance. We were about a mile away and 500 ft off shore, going very slowly with the broken piece of mast as a paddle. To make things a little exciting a four foot shark broke water about twenty feet away from us making everyone a little nervous. We started laughing about our predicament, since we were all Coast Guard sailors and were supposed to have things like oars, life jackets, signal flares and running lights! It was dark now and our main worry was that we didn't have a light to show our position and the inter-island passenger ship would soon be leaving the harbor. We could hear the liner getting ready to leave as she signaled, with her whistle that she was backing out of her berth! Since we were in the channel by then we started paddling like mad to get out of the path of that ship which we knew would be coming out pretty fast and at night they wouldn't be able to see us!

We were now on the other side of the channel about 200 feet or so when I noticed that the lights of the city were going up and down about 10 feet, I yelled my concern about this just as I heard a noise loud and clear which sounded just like a breaker on the beach as it curls over and pounds the sand. All three of us began back paddling like frenzy before we got caught in a breaker which could have tossed us up on the beach, wrecked and mangled. This was the out side of Sand Island, the outer side of the harbor. We made it back to the channel and figured that it would be safe to make our way in as the ferry had left and there wasn't much chance of a big ship coming out now so close to midnight! When we got back to the pier where our ship was tied up there was a group waiting for us, full of questions. Of course we had to tell them what had happened and everyone agreed that we were lucky to get off as easily as we did! The ship's carpenter from the work shop at the light house facility offered to repair our mast, an offer we accepted gladly. We found out that the guy wire clamps on the rigging were the cause of the mast breaking when the pressure of the coming about maneuver was put on it.

The next day, I went into the work shop at the pier looking for the carpenter's mate, I found him working on a project for an officer from another ship. I asked him if he could repair our mast, like new? He said he thought he could fix it like new but that he couldn't work on it till later.

About a week later he called me over to the shop and said he had the mast ready, I looked at it and told him it looked great. We put it back on the sailboat and this time we made sure the guy's or stay's would hold!

The radio shack needed to be re-arranged, so the captain told me to draw up plans to scale on the changes we needed to make for a better operation. Now I thought, "I'm going to be in deep trouble," as all I had was six month's of mechanical drawing in high school. So I started out bravely showing the changes we were thinking about and I sent them into the Navy Engineering Office for approval, knowing that they would come back with some kind of nasty inquiry as to who made this drawing? To my surprise they sent an approval on my drawing, so we went ahead and started to make the changes. After talking to the carpenter's mate, from the repair shop about what we needed, he suggested that we use a large piece of Philippine mahogany for our operating position, which we all agreed was a good idea. It worked out well as a desk top and looked like a beautiful piece of furniture, especially after we waxed and polished it. The radio shack was now outfitted and arranged so that two operators could be quartered there.

We also had gotten orders to black out antenna insulator glass that might leak light. We had one glass insulator that would leak light to the outside, so the Navy sent us a can of insulation paint that would block out light but not interfere with our transmitted signal to the big antenna we rigged between the two mast's on the ship. We had to paint the inside and out side of the insulator so as to not have it touch the high powered radio frequency signal path to the antenna.

Chapter 4.

Medical Helper.

The time was about August of 1940 and I had worn out my first issue of dress shoes, so off I went to get a new pair of black regulation dress shoes. My feet weren't made to fit the sizes that small stores, (the Navy/Coast Guard supply depot), had in stock so I made do on what they had. The end result was that I had developed a nice blister on my right heel. One of my friends looked at my blister and said, "Let me pop that for you, I've had experience in the art of first aid." So he proceeded to lance the

35

blister with a safety razor blade. The blister was drained and we put a band-aid over the wound. You see, we didn't have any medical personnel on board, so we had to make do. About two days later, when I got out of bed, I noticed that my right leg felt kind of funny, like I had springs in my leg when I'd stamp the deck with it. I looked at my leg and saw that there were red streaks running up almost to my knee! Since we were docked at pier Four, I went to the captain and requested permission to see a pharmacist at the first aid station across the street from us. I hobbled over there and the pharmacist mate took one look and told me that I had to go to the Naval Hospital in Pearl Harbor immediately! So I hobbled back to the ship across the street and told the captain what the pharmacist had told me. He had a hard time believing me but finally was convinced and told me to go on my own transportation to the hospital. I went down on the dock and found a yard worker who had access to the old Chevy pickup truck that was used for errands by all the ships tied up at pier Four. We drove out to Pearl Harbor Hospital and I went into the reception desk to explain my problem, showing my leg full of red streaks to a pharmacist mate on duty at the desk. He took one look and said "You get to bed in ward B-3 this minute," "I said, where is the bath room, I need to go," "He said forget that, your going to bed now!" So off to bed I went, that is when I learned what a duct was! A doctor came in to look at my leg within a few minutes. They put a heat lamp over my foot and gave me a new drug called Sulfanilamide, that's what it sound like to me anyway. On my second day of treatment, who should show up for treatment in B-3 ward but my friend Scott! He told me that he had an attack of appendicitis while at sea on board the Taney, so they put him on board the China Clipper at Midway

Island and flew him back here to Pearl Harbor. We conversed with each other through the use of morse code, using our hands as if they were blinker lights as we had both been studying morse code and all the other ways to transmit messages, like using flags, etc. We got pretty proficient at this so we gave each; other the information as to why we were in the hospital. We used this method of communications because we were across the room from each other. It was a pleasant surprise to be in the Navy hospital at the same time, even though we both had serious illnesses. As we began recovering they moved Scott and me to another ward. We discovered that we were the only patients in the ward, so with nothing to do we would make up our beds, get dressed, hide our medical charts under our pillows and wander around the hospital grounds which was just across the entrance channel fro Ford Island. There was a park bench sitting by the sidewalk situated so that we could view ships coming in the channel and planes like PBY's practice their take off's and landings. We tired of that after one day and since no one was monitoring our ward we decided to sneak into town as we both still had our liberty passes in our wallets. While we visited around our ships at pier 12 and pier 4 my skipper spotted me and said if you don't return by tomorrow I'm tossing your seabag out on the dock! All I could say, "Yes sir! I'll try sir!" We then thought that maybe he · would be calling the naval hospital asking about me, so we dashed back to Pearl got to our ward and placed our charts back in place and I went looking for the guy who had sent us to the new ward. When I found him, I told him of my problem, to make it more dramatic, I said my ship was leaving the area the next day and since the problem of my leg was cured, could he get my release from the hospital that day. He said, "Sorry but we release patients only on

Friday." This was on a Wednesday. But he added, "get me your charts and I will see what I can do." When he looked at our charts, he turned white, because there were no entries for a whole week on them. He began filling in data as if we checked every day, covering the fact that they had forgotten all about our being there. The doctor in charge of the ward heard our story about our ships leaving and gave us both our releases, so we left, that Wednesday for our respective ships. Scott's ship was now the Tiger and I was still on the Kukui. The war news getting more heavy now! The U.S. started the draft that I had avoided by joining the Coast Guard early. Germany was bombing London and Japan was fighting in China and expanding else where! One day while I was downtown Honolulu, I ran into a bunch of National Guard troopers, who were on their way to the Philippines, one of them asked me where he could find a telephone, as he wanted to phone home! I said, "how rich are you, it's going to cost plenty, you're in the Hawaiian Islands and to phone the states is very expensive. To my surprise he didn't know he was in Hawaii! I don't know if he tried but wondered about the National Guard troops being sent to the Philippines. The news on the war in Europe wasn't very good and it looked as if we were getting tougher on trade with Japan. On one mail call day I got a nasty letter from my draft board in Mill Valley, Ca. Of course it was mailed to my folks address and my sister forwarded it to me along with a letter saying maybe I should go talk to the draft board! I thought it was a good idea as they said that if I didn't come in and sign up for the draft they would throw me in jail! So, I went to the skipper and told him that I had to go back to the states cause I had a problem with the draft board and they wanted to talk to me. All I got was a dirty look from him and we both started laughing over it. He said, "nice try Swede," my nick name at the time, and that ended my chance to get a trip home!

All this time while working as a radioman on this tender, we were changing buoys and fixing and renewing gas bottles on all the automatic lights and replacing burnt out lamps on range lights and surveying sites for new markers. We climbed up towers too and had to work one handed, one hand for yourself and one for the work! I even carved my initials in the lamp cage of the rear range light at one harbor entrance, it's probably still there inside the lamp cage at one hundred feet high! By now I was the only radioman on board. My trainer had departed for the states as soon as I made my rating. Since there was only one man at the radio position, we were allowed to stand our watch by using the loud speaker twenty four hours a day and log things only important to us. This allowed me to be able to handle traffic for our ship when it was broadcast and the rest of the time I could roam around the ship or do what ever I wanted to do, within the range of the loud speaker, of course. It was good duty!

We headed out of Honolulu channel. Our destination was Maui, on the Lahina side of the Island. We had a load of mooring buoys, old fashion anchors and lots of chain to fasten the mooring buoys and anchors together a navy tug was working with us, as we were going to set up an anchorage area for navy ships about a mile offshore in what they called Lahina Roads. After setting three of these moorings we got a call from the navy tug asking us if they could have swim call, it was a very hot afternoon. We turned them down as we wanted to get this job done as quickly as we could. They acted very put out that we turned them down as the clear cool water looked very inviting. That night as I was wandering around the lower deck, I saw our cook standing near the railing with his white hat in his hand holding on to a chalk line that was running through his hat and singing loudly like a buzzzzz, then it stopped. Then he would start pulling the line up leaving a pile on the deck, then all of a sudden it would buzzzzzz again as the line ran through his white hat! I asked, "What in the world are you doing?" He said, "Believe it or not I have a big shark on this line, I baited a big hook with some old beef and hooked this shark and it keeps diving till it hits bottom, then lets me pull it all the way to the surface and when it hits the surface it dives back to the bottom." "Aren't you afraid you'll get caught in the line, I asked?" He said, "Naw," The line was singing through his white hat in his hand, as the shark was diving to the bottom again! It was about 20 fathoms deep at this spot, (about hundred and twenty feet deep). We thought maybe we should get a gun and shoot this shark as he wasn't giving up by the way of his running up and down on the line. One crew member saw what was going on and went for his 22 pistol. The next time the cook pulled the shark to the surface the guy with the pistol fired a couple of shots into the head of the shark. The shark dove down to the bottom again and didn't seem affected by the shots so the next time he broke the surface the shooter put two more shots to the head, with no apparent effect. Soon the shark started to slow down and we managed to throw a lasso over his tail, with a heavy 2 inch size line. We then woke up the winch operator, explained that we wanted to haul a shark up on deck as he was too big to do it by hand. He agreed to help, so we winched him up on the deck, and with awe, saw that we were fooling around with a shark twelve and a half feet in length, weighing at least 500 lbs and had mouth twenty inches wide. We left him hanging and I was going to cut the whole jaw out with all the teeth intact in the morning. In the morning it was quite a sight to see the huge shark hanging there, from the boom derrick. One of the first things we did was signal the tug crew and asked them if they wanted to go swimming. Needless to say, we didn't even get an answer. So I started to work on getting the jaw bone out when I noticed that all the teeth had been removed by various members of the crew! So I dismissed the thought of removing the jaw bone. We dumped the poor shark over board that morning.

As far as using this area as a fleet anchorage, I don't think it was ever used. I think that they, (Navy brass), thought that keeping a lot of ships like the carriers out of Pearl Harbor, where they could be trapped and bottled up for days, they would be much safer anchored on the open sea! I wondered why this plan wasn't carried out. I read later on, that it was the old Battle Ship Admirals who balked at any changes being made that didn't fit in with their battle ship strategies.

We were working in the Maui Island area where the lava flow comes right down to the water's edge. We were surveying our markers and automatic lights on the shore line. The whole area looked like a huge potato patch that had just been ploughed. We took the work boat in on the shore line and jumped off onto the lava beds to begin our work on some of the automatic equipment. This was an extra job for the radioman, working on the electrical systems. After about an hours work we became very thirsty, so I tried signaling the ship to send us some water but I never got them to understand what I was trying to get them to do! After that we made sure we had water with us when we worked in those isolated places. The next day we motored into a neat little cove and the survey gang got out and left me to watch the boat. It was a very picturesque scene with a brook tumbling into a deep water hole where I could see many beautiful tiny colored tropical fish swimming about in this deep water hole, I've never seen such a colorful display of tropical fish. There were many Samoan coconut trees along the sandy waters edge. There was one tree that had a trunk that curved out almost horizontally before it started up towards the sky. This tree had a bunch of large coconuts that looked as if they would be easy to get to. As I had plenty of time on my hands I decided to climb this tree since I could walk halfway up the tree before having to climb it like a native. It looked so easy but when I got to the vertical part I found that I had to shinny up as when I was a kid climbing trees. It was tough climbing and when I got to the area where the coconuts were I hardly had the strength to hang on and twist a coconut around until it broke away from it's mooring. It was a lot tougher and seemed to hang in there as if it didn't want to let loose but finally dropped to the sand below and I slid down the horizontal part and jumped to the beach. Now I had a coconut but how could I get that tough husk off so as to get the milk and nut parts. I had to wait for the work party to come back before I could do anything with my prize. One of the work party happened to be Hawaiian and he had that husk off quick as a wink, it's all in the know how! Being a native Hawaiian it was a simple operation for him, he just found a sharp piece of lava and slammed the coconut into it and opened it up enough where he could rip off the husk easily. We all had a swig of the coconut milk which was sweet and refreshing. The whole episode would have been forgotten, but for me, I had skin burns on both shins which lasted about two weeks. That was the last time I ever tried to climb a coconut tree!

Back at Pier Four I was getting pretty efficient at operating the radio shack and between the GCT time ticks for our chronometer corrections and copying the monthly officer promotions, some one in the district office decided I should be transferred to our shore station NMO. This was a big deal for me and I was happy to there, I never thought I would be stationed ashore. Before I left for this new assignment, which would happen when my replacement showed up, the supply officer came into the radio room and told me to make up a list of supplies that the radio department would need, as it was near the fiscal year an time to order every thing for the year. He also said order twice as much as we would need, since they always cut it in half anyway. So, I did just that and sent in a big order for antenna wire, insulators and everything I could think of. Before my replacement showed up, my inventory list of replacement parts showed up first. They sent everything I had listed, nothing was missing. We had to find a place to store it all since I really didn't need all of that order immediately. We realized that since the war clouds were getting closer the supply department wasn't cutting down on any orders. Lucky for us there was room on Pier Four to store all of this inventory. My replacement showed up one afternoon after that, I got pretty excited about this turn of events and was busily showing him the whole operation. I explained the watch schedule and showed him how the high frequency transmitter worked. After showing him everything I immediately got my belongings together and left for Diamond Head Light House where the radio station NMO was located.

Chapter 5.

The Second Oath!

When I got to Diamond Head I was introduced to all hands by the radio chief who was in charge. I was told that I would have a regular watch covering all Coast Guard bands and the commercial bands on 600 meters (500kcs). I was to share a room with three other radioman, Tony Silva, B. Lesko and A. Bell, they were all third class radioman. Before I could settle in, the communication for officer for the 14th Naval District H.M. Anthony Chief Warrant Officer came out to the station and told me I had to take a second oath. I had to raise my right hand and swear that I would never reveal what I was about to see or do to any one. The penalty would be life imprisonment in a Federal Prison. This was a very serious oath to which I was saying "I do." Chief Warrant Anthony told me that I was to study the Japanese code system and get proficient in copying this code, which he called "Orange Code." This was the first time I had ever heard of such codes and believe me, I took it all in very seriously! Besides doing my regular chores of standing watches I began studying Orange code characters. There were four positions in the operating room for copying this code. They had special Underwood typewriters with the Japanese code characters on each of the keys. After a few weeks of practice I was beginning to get the hang of it when an old timer by the name of Bill Corey, gave me a bit of advice. He said, 'Son if you get good at copying this code, you'll never get out of here till your enlistment is up." That didn't bother me, since it was a nice assignment and the food was excellent, besides we were within walking distance to Waikiki Beach. Tony Silva and I became good friends and we would go on liberty together. One night we were cruising around the bars in the Waikiki area. We were having fun but decided it was time to go back to station. It must have been about 10 PM when we arrived to see all the lights on and much activity going on with Mr. Anthony in charge. He spotted us as we came through the kitchen door and commanded us to help them. There's a floating dry dock and tug boat in trouble, Larsen you man the direction finder and Tony help me over here by me." I jumped immediately on to the direction finder instrument and yelled to them, "I'm on, what's the call sign of the tug?" Mr. Anthony yelled back, "will you get a reading please," I couldn't hear a signal at the time, so in desperation I spun the wheel of the direction finder antenna around and gave the reading where the indicator stopped, all the while he was looking at me. I thought, "Oh I'm in trouble now but maybe I can blame it on the drinks I had while on liberty!" All of a sudden he started laughing and said, "It's alright son I just wanted you to get a little practice on the direction finder, we already know where they are, they are 500 miles west of Panama in a fierce storm with waves as high as ninety feet." The dry dock has twelve men aboard and the tug cannot find her. "We were activating a search task force but the tug said, "No" as they hadn't sent an SOS and they were afraid of the mariner law that any abandoned vessel is up for grabs if found and towed to safety. About three days later we heard the tug found the floating dry dock and that the crew aboard her had been contact with the home office in New York by high frequency radio telephone. We never found out where they were headed but wondered why no one told us about them talking to the New York office?

I knew we were getting closer to war when we were put on special assignment to keep track of Aussie pilots flying lend lease PBY'S, the US Navy Catalina flying boats, they were in transit between Hawaii and Canton Island. While on that assignment I would talk to them on their way there. The Aussie accent was something I thought I could have some fun with, so I started mimicking them. Their response was rather brisk and unfriendly. I took the hint and didn't try it again. During the month of September we were issued NAV/CG liberty cards and were told that we were now under the US Navy's jurisdiction which meant that their shore patrol police would be the one that would watch our behavior while on liberty. It also meant that all the Coast Guard personnel was now Navy.

Another indication that we were ready for war, was the radio dills we had with all the armed forces, the Navy, the Army Air Force, the Army, and the Marines! Every group used different types of special signals, making it difficult to co-ordinate the operation's, so we never came to any satisfactory work out. These drills died out in a few days. I often wondered about the outcome from these drills but the war came on before I heard anything on the subject. I guess the higher ups may have had some reaction but it never filtered down to the troops.

One sunny day my friend Scott and I decided to take a plane ride. We had the old Studebaker, so we drove out to John Rogers Airport. It is located west of Hickham Field. We inquired about the fare and was told that the two of us could go up for a ride for three dollars. We thought that was fair enough so we said "OK." The pilot pointed to an old looking bi-plane, vintage World War One and said,

"Climb aboard in the back cockpit there's room for both of you!" So we did as he sat in the front cockpit and started the engine, warmed it up a bit and soon started down the runway. This was a big thrill for me, it was the first time I had ever been in an airplane. The pilot made sure we had our seat belts well fastened before we started, which caused me a some what anxious period, I thought he was going to do the loop or something like a barrel roll but so far we just kept climbing into the sky. As we leveled off I began to take in the scenery, it was a beautiful cloudless day and you could see for miles, we skirted the edge of the beach on our way past Waikiki Beach. We then swerved to the left and circled over Diamond Head, right over my station NMO at the light house. This was great, I had a view of my place from an airplane! We must have been at least two thousand feet in altitude, when all of a sudden the plane took a sharp dive for about two seconds, we went straight down then leveled off and headed back to the John Rogers Airport. I guess he wanted to give us a little thrill with that dive and he did. We landed very easily and drifted to a stop right in front of the hanger where we started. We jumped out and thanked the pilot for the good ride and headed home thinking that it would be fun to take flying lessons soon. This was around the 21st of November 1941!

We drove back to town and had a couple of beers before back to our stations. When I got back to the radio station the chief in charge told me that a warrant officer was going to come out and give me a test for the radioman second class rating. This meant that I was going to get some theory testing and some speed testing on the Morse Code! So I went around to all the old timers trying to find out what this officer would be throwing at me in the way of a test? He came out to the station a few days later and started to give me a quiz on electronics that I never studied and barely knew existed, so he went back to the district office in down town Honolulu, with the recommendation that I not be promoted. I wondered about the reason for the test and figured that Chief Warrant Anthony was the one who recommended it because of my action during the lost dry dock action. It probably made an imprint of me on his brain, forgetting how I did, but remembering me!

In this month of November of 1941, we went through several major black out drills with the whole civilian population participating in the drills. During this time we received orders from headquarters to have a fully loaded pistol, a Colt 45 automatic, at each of our operating positions. This puzzled most of us at the station. This order started many rumors and many arguments on our chances of getting of getting into the war. One morning while discussing the chances of getting into the war, Bill Corey, an old timer who was one of the experienced Orange Code copier's, expressed the opinion that, "We would win the war with Japan within two weeks." My reply to his opinion was, "We would be lucky if we could win a war with them in two years." He looked at me as if I were some kind of traitor, to say something like that, so I explained to him that I based my theory on what I had seen about Japanese ships in the British published book, Janes Fighting Ships. Which covered all the major nations naval fighting ships. This book gave all the specifics on each ship such as tonnage, armament, speed, profile, horse power, number of screws and personnel In the section of Japanese ships I remember several pages with data on their battleships and cruisers, saying that it was believed that it was so many feet long and had certain size guns and believed to have a speed of about 33 knots, they managed to build ships secretly, which proved to me that we didn't know how strong their military forces were. His reaction to my reasoning was that I was talking traitorously and that I wasn't loyal to my country! I quit trying to make him see my point of view and dropped the subject entirely to keep peace between us.

The district office always forwarded all warning or directives to our station, so that we would be up to compliance with what was happening in the area. One important one came as a warning from the Army saying that there were reasons to expect saboteur action from fifth columnists in the Hawaiian area. This warning explained the reason for the Colt automatic pistol at every operating position.

On my operating position, covering the Merchant Marine calling frequencies, I was getting more and more emergency signals from ships under attack by German submarines or enemy aircraft, one example was the SS Steel Mariner, a USA registered vessel, sent out the new distress signal SSS SSS SSS, which meant I'm being attacked by a submarine. This signal was heard on 600 meters or 500 khrtz, the commercial emergency distress frequency. The ship sunk in the Red Sea that night while sending that message! The frequency of 600 meters carries well at night and that signal carried more than half way around the world. This new distress call was put into use so that there was a definite difference between an accidental sinking and a vessel being attacked by an enemy ship or plane. There were many of this type of signal heard in the far Pacific area also. Copying them was disturbing. I began to have the feeling that we were going to war soon.

Chapter 6.

December 6th, 1941.

It was a lazy Saturday and we had a simple inspection, nothing like on board ship. During the afternoon I lounged around in the back yard taking in the warm sunshine and caught up on some reading. After a hearty dinner I got ready to go on my regular watch at 8 PM. It started out uneventfully. The CAA weather station out of Hilo, Hawaii, came in right on time. There was nothing unusual about the report, just the regular readings, temperature, barometer, wind direction and velocity, and dew point. Everything appeared to be normal for this time of year. Since we were in the night cycle on this watch where the lower frequency's carry a very long way, we began to hear the powerful West Coast commercial stations from Seattle, Washington to the Panama Canal Zone loud and clear. The Seattle commercial station could be heard calling the merchant ship Cynthia Olsen, saying that they had an important message for her! After the initial call was made and there was no response, the rest of the commercial stations up and down the West Coast began repeating the call for her to answer, this included a call from us. This was all done on the calling frequency 600 meters. This was standard procedure just in case the ship was out of the range of the original calling station The Cynthia Olsen was never contacted and to this day she is listed as lost at sea! It was speculated that the Cynthia Olsen may have run in to the Japanese Pearl

Harbor Raiders and sunk before she could spread the alarm but that was only speculation. The other version was that her cargo of lumber shifted in rough weather causing her to capsize. Later in the night around midnight there were lots of weak unidentified signals, in fact I thought I heard an SOS but it was too weak for me to verify. Just about that time my relief came on, as it was close to the end of my watch, so I briefed him on the what I was hearing and we both surmised that it could be a China coast fishing boat, a foreign airplane or even an old tramp steamer off the coast of China. The transmitting signals had the same characteristics as most of the Japanese transmitters, which is something that you recognize when you work out on the Pacific Rim area.

Before turning in we both discussed a few of the evenings events such as hearing those strange signals, the Cynthia Olsen not answering her call and that we hadn't heard any Japanese passenger or freighter vessels since the luxury liner Nita Maru had left Honolulu three days before. We also talked about the Navy using our regular Coast Guard channel for their harbor patrol channel. We never got an official notice of their using our channel, which bothered us a lot because it interfered with working our ships at times. It was time to turn in for the night, it was about 2:15 AM on December 7th, 1941!!

Chapter 7.

Sunday December 7th.

About 7:55 AM I was rudely awakened by the rattling of all the bedroom windows. My first thought was that it felt like an earthquake, the building was shaking and there were loud rumbling sounds like heavy thunder! Then I heard sounds like heavy firing of guns. As I started to get up, I thought what a day to start war games on, it's Sunday, don't they have any sense at all? It's just like the Army to pull a stunt like this, of course the Navy was in on the act too. Just about that time my watch partner, who had relieved me at 2 AM, came rushing into the bedroom exclaiming that the USS Ward had depth charged a submarine just off of Barbers Point at about 6 AM. He said he picked up the message cause it was sent on our frequency 2670 (our high frequency main channel) but was sent to NPM the Navy radio shore station. I asked him if he sent that message to our downtown head quarters and he replied "No I didn't because it was sent to NPM." I told him he should have sent it into our office just to keep his watch covered. Since we knew Anthony was in on that kind of stuff. As I was getting dressed I heard faint sounds of airplane engines. I quickly dashed out of the room, ran through the kitchen and out the back door just in time to see 3 planes fly over the house at about 500 feet above me. They were flying in formation and I could see big red dots on their wings. I watched them flying in the direction of down town Honolulu and in line with going to Pear Harbor! I ran in the house and told everyone, "Three Army planes flew over the house, I know they weren't Navy planes so they must be Army planes because they had big red dots under their wings as some sort of disguise for war games. Looking out towards Pearl Harbor I could see huge clouds of smoke billowing up into the sky and it looked like a bunch of planes were zooming around Hickham Field and Pearl Harbor. Since this action came as a big surprise, I wondered if the military brass were trying to see what our reaction would be by throwing this surprise drill. Just about that time Chief Kerns, our man in charge that day, told me to cover the harbor channel and the commercial channel till we found out what is going on. Since we had an excellent view of the Pearl Harbor channel entrance from the operating position where I was operating, I could see any ships coming out of the Pearl Harbor channel entrance. Looking through that particular window I observed a destroyer running very slowly towards the open sea. She was not making much head way and seemed to be blowing white smoke out of her single stack which I took to mean that it hadn't quite got enough boiler pressure to go full speed. Suddenly a huge geyser of water erupted just a few yards off her stern. I didn't know if she had dropped a depth charge or if there was a plane bombing her. This started us to wondering if this was a make believe war game or was it the real thing? I thought that if this was the real thing I wanted no part of it! At about 8:30 AM Chief Kerns sent my partner Tony Silva downtown to our headquarters with all of last nights logs and message. He was to find out what was going on? He took the panel truck, our official vehicle, drove fast as he could on Kapolanai Boulevard to our district office down town. During this time I was busy logging everything I heard on

2670 kcs and 500 kcs (kcs now known as hrz). The first thing I heard was a distress call from a commercial sport fishing boat on 2670 our Coast Guard frequency. The caller sounded very excited and said "some Army Air Force pilot has gone berserk and is shooting at us with his machine guns and had hit them." An Army Colonel, who was a guest on his vessel was wounded." He gave his location as just off of Barbers Point. He pleaded with us to do something about it. We acknowledge his message and passed it on to our down town headquarters by teletype. He also informed us that the boat was disabled and was sinking. I looked out of our window facing north, where we could see the mouth of the entrance channel to Pearl Harbor and the Barber's Point area but couldn't see the fishing boat. After watching that destroyer getting bombed and the fishing boat getting strafed, this started us wondering if this was a real war or a drill, the time was now about 8:30 AM. In the kitchen you could hear a radio on low volume, playing heavy military marches or martial music. Then an announcement was made that we were being attacked by an unidentified enemy air force. We still hadn't got any official notice from Headquarters, but we figured that it had to be the Japanese Navy! Just about then I was looking out the west window where I could see the Diamond Head buoy, (that was used to mark the end of the race for sailing boats from the West Coast to Hawaii), a tremendous set of geysers came out of the sea and shot about fifty or sixty feet in the air. It looked as they were about 500 yards from the shore. I held my breath expecting shells to come bouncing or skipping right up to our building thinking that they were made by a salvo of heavy shells from a cruiser or a battle ship that was lurking just over the horizon and trying to find the correct range and would be firing more shells at us any minute but when I didn't see any skipping along the way after the original geysers I figured that it must have been three bombs dropped from some plane at a high altitude and the wind pushed them out past Diamond Head. It could have been that they were dropped by accident or maybe the pilot dropped them because he was about to return to his ship and didn't want to have his load of bombs on board when he landed on his carrier. Later it was rumored that some of the cruisers were firing their six and eight inch batteries at the planes, but that was just hearsay, the geysers I saw shot up too straight for shell type impact. More emergency radio telephone messages were coming in on channel 2670 kcs. The first one I worked was an unidentified station calling NMO, our call sign, saying that there were two destroyers sinking off of Kaneohe Bay. I asked for a station identification but they didn't answer my query. Rather than pursue that line of action I got on the regular Coast Guard land line to Makapau Light House and talked to the station keeper, asking him if he could see anything that looked like two destroyers or ships in the area of Kaneohe Bay or out to sea near there? He answered, "negative," saying that he had a good view of Kaneohe Bay and the open sea and he saw no activity out there. Since he couldn't see any action we figured that it had to be some fifth columnist group trying to sabotage our operation! At this time we realized that we should have some kind of system that would make sure we were working with a friendly military station, like a coded signal for the day. We had been trying out some practice on this kind of operation but those in charge didn't think it was wise to try anything like that at this time since there was plenty of confusion already. Around 11:00 AM a local radio station sent out a warning that there might be a chance that the enemy had dropped poison into some of our drinking water reservoir's! I quickly ran into the bath room and filled our bath tub up with as much water as it could hold, just in case the story was true. I got back to my operating position just as a skipper of a mine sweeper called his commanding officer on 2670 kcs, the Navy harbor frequency, our Coast Guard channel, with this message, "Sir should I keep sweeping the harbor channel even though my cutter blade has broken off?" The answer was "No, come in and get it repaired, God damn it." Right after that I heard a quick "Yes sir," along with some engine noise and shouting in the back ground with a little bit of swearing, evidently the microphone button was stuck in the on position, then I heard a loud voice yell "The mike is still keying." With that I heard a definite click as they finally shut the mike off. It was a good thing that it did shut off cause no one could get through that transmission to communicate their own messages. Now the Matson line, the Lurline, was calling us, NMO on 500 kcs, asking what was going on? She was calling us in Morse Code, known as CW in the commercial radio lingo, before I go any further on this, I have to admit that the Matson line ship could have been the Matsonia, her sister passenger ship. Anyway, she asked me what was going on? I called the Chief over and asked him, "What should I tell them?" He said, "To play it safe, say that we are being attacked by unidentified enemy planes," which I did, just in case they weren't Japanese! I also gave her the code signal QRT to stay off the air do not transmit any more! With that they gave me an R, for receipt and shut down. They were out at least 14 hours from Honolulu on their way to San Francisco. Hopefully there were no enemy submarines near them. At around 10 AM the second run of bombers came in and continued their devastating havoc. My watch partner, Tony Silva, had just made it back from his down town run to our district headquarters. He told us that he had to dodge bomb craters in the road and had a rough time driving. He also said that there were many civilian casualties. Looking over towards Pearl Harbor we could see huge columns of black smoke billowing up into the sky. We could feel the concussion and hear the explosions from this second attack. We wondered how many sailors, marines, soldiers and civilians were killed or wounded. We could see airplanes zooming and diving around, some could have been ours fighting back but they were too far away to really tell. I heard later on that only about six or seven planes got off the ground to retaliate that day. I recorded a call from a group of B17 bombers from Hamilton Field, California asking us or any one where they could land. We didn't work them but I thought they should have tried Maui because Hickham field was right next door to Pearl Harbor and probably was getting strafed and bombed also. From what we could see from our position, it looked as if the casualty count was going to be quite high and the destruction would be astronomical! The time was now close to noon and Chief Kerns, the officer in charge of the station for this day, decided that since we didn't have any security at all, that there should be a guard on duty on the premises from now on. Since I the junior petty officer at the station he chose me for that duty, handing me a 45 Colt automatic hand gun, two clips of shells and a full box of extra shells. The order was to cover the area around the station and make sure that there were no intruders lurking around the premises. Since I was wearing dungarees already, I just added my dungaree jacket which had large pockets that could accommodate my extra box of ammo and the extra clip. Now I felt I was ready for any invasion force that came rushing up from the beach! I figured, if there were an invasion tonight and we couldn't hold them off, who ever they were, I could at least have a fighting chance by heading up over Diamond Head and disappearing into the mountains and continue fighting on my own. Just as I was stepping outside to start my guard duty, I heard our chief commissary steward, first class cook Brady, (One of the first black men to attain a regular rating rather than an officer's steward rating), mumble to himself, "Damn it, I was going to have Kentucky Southern fried chicken today for our Sunday dinner but things are too upsetting to do that kind of a meal now." The whole crew had lost any desire to eat except to consume many cups of coffee. We all agreed with the chief, who the hell cares about eating when things look as bad as this did! I couldn't believe that I was now in a war, even though we had no official notice yet, we realized that it was so. The first thing I did as I stepped out side to begin my guard duty was to glance seaward, to see if there were any warships on the horizon, a natural reaction for me, as this was the west side of the Island. The next thing I decided to do was to check out the area's around the building looking for things that might hinder or help me as I had the guard duty for the entire night with no relief. While checking out the perimeter of the area I noticed a convoy of Army trucks with soldiers in full combat gear on go by the station. Since we were on the main road that leads to Koko Head on the south end of the Island, I watched the convoy progress down the road and saw that they were going to set up camp at an old searchlight platform located in that area below the road. I kept that in mind, thinking that I didn't want some trigger happy soldier shooting at me in the middle of the night.

It got dark very early it seemed to me and we were now under martial law and we were to have a total black out until further notice. I began marching around the premises with my 45 automatic in my hand, rather than having it in my holster, because I wanted to be ready to fire it immediately if need be. There was a shell in the chamber waiting to be fired and I felt ready for anything. Of course I had the safety engaged since the trigger was touchy and I was very nervous. I circled the house a couple of times, then looked over the hedge down the embankment towards the waters edge thinking I might see a landing barge or a surf boat or what ever the enemy would use, expecting to see a bunch of Japanese infantry soldiers armed to the teeth and getting ready to take over the Island. Rumors had been flying around all day that the Japanese Navy was just over the horizon waiting for darkness to fall before starting their invasion! With darkness upon us my imagination was really running wild now! I had heard that the Coast Guard had been doing a lot of experimenting with different types of surf boats and landing craft, so I assumed that the Japanese Navy was doing the same thing. I wondered if the US Navy or Army had done any studies on this same kind of activity. Since I didn't read any accounts of this type of action in any of our journals, I assumed that there wasn't any training of this kind by our military forces. But, there was a question in my mind that maybe the Japanese Navy or Army had done some training in this field, since they pulled off this raid without so much as a gentlemen's notice of going to war. They could have been training for this phase of the operation for months and had the landing phase down to perfection. So every small bush and shrub in the dark became a potential Japanese invader! Looking towards Waikiki Beach I could see some lights on and wondered who the dummies were who didn't shut them off. Soon I could hear shots being fired near that area. I could hear yelling and figured it must be the MP'S shouting at people to put out their lights. Later on, one of our officers told me that the MP'S had come into his apartment complex and broke into the apartment below his apartment and since there was no one home, shot out the lights. What made him kind of unhappy about the incident was the fact that the bullets went through the floor into his bedroom narrowly missing him as he was sleeping. I heard sporadic gun fire going on all through the night. I could understand why there was so much firing because in the darkness I imagined I saw enemy soldiers hiding behind every bush or tree on the hill side below us. I still had the feeling that the whole Japanese fleet was just over the horizon launching their small boats full of mean, nasty soldiers and I had to be ready for the encounter, I was one nervous sailor!

Around 10:00 PM I went inside the house to grab a cup of coffee. I took it out side to our little alcove near the kitchen where we had a table and some wicker chairs to lounge in. It seemed to me that the enemy was not going to invade tonight, still I wondered why they had attacked so viciously and hadn't followed up with an invasion plan which seemed to be the logical thing to do? After lighting a cigarette with my trusty Zippo lighter shielding the flare of the lighter with the palms of my hands, of course, I sat down in one of the wicker chairs to enjoy my cup of coffee and my smoke. Just as I finished my coffee and was stubbing out my smoke I heard several loud rifle or revolver shots that seemed to be coming from the south side of our area, they were loud enough to be very close to our perimeter! It was apparent that the shots came from the area where I had seen the soldiers setting up a station at the old search light platform which was a relic from World War One. As I walked cautiously to the area where the shots came from, to check out if it were really those soldiers shooting at shadows I came across two of our crew members vigorously digging what appeared to be a fox hole right in the middle of our well groomed lawn! They were digging very rapidly and looked rather nervous. I asked them what was going on, they both stopped digging and stared at me, saying in unison, "We heard shots and thought that maybe you were shot!" They sent a message to the district office down town that you had been shot and that you were either wounded or killed by enemy gun fire! I asked, "Since I haven't been shot what can I do to help in this situation?" One said, "I think that we are being attacked by invaders." Pretending to believe them, even though I knew that it was probably the soldiers next door, I said I would check along and around the front gate entrance which was just off the highway running past our location. This is the road that runs past Diamond Head and continues on towards Black Point and Koko Head. I said, "I'll see if I can spot any action while up there," so I bravely left them still digging the fox hole and headed for the front entrance. By now I was convinced that it was our friends next door, so I wasted little time looking around the entrance and head back to the fox hole. When I got there I told them that there isn't anyone around and that I thought it could be the group of soldiers below us at the old search light location just to the south of us. I said, "Those soldiers are as nervous as everyone else, they probably saw some movement in the bushes when a little breeze came up and started shooting thinking maybe they were really seeing enemy soldiers coming up the hill from the beach." The two crew members quit digging the fox hole and went inside the house to tell everyone that I was OK and that there wasn't any force invading the compound. About fifteen minutes later I saw the early evening watch-standers, who normally went to their respective home, take blankets and pillows into the old light house for a night of sleep, since there was no way they could drive home because of the blackout. It was impossible to drive around the roads in total darkness and they hadn't figured out how to adjust the headlights on automobiles. Most of these operators were married and were living on subsistence and housing allowances because there wasn't enough space to house all the personnel at the station.

Around midnight I started looking down the slope of the embankment towards the beach trying to see if I could spot any landing craft or fifth columnist group creeping up through the bushes towards me. The more I studied the bushes and the terrain the more I realized I was getting paranoid about this guard duty. I was crouching slightly looking down toward the beach behind the hedge about ten feet from the back porch door when I heard the door swing open and saw someone peeking out at me. I heard this person suddenly groan and saying no! No! No!. I recognized the person and yelled really loud, "For chriss sake Bill it's only me on guard duty relax." That calmed him down, then he turned around and closed the door and went back into the main part of the house. We never ever discussed that encounter again. This was the guy that I had the argument with about winning a war with Japan, I wondered what he was thinking of now? The rest of the night was uneventful until until about dawn. It was getting light enough to see a long ways out to sea. The sky was clear and I didn't see anything that looked like a ship, especially a Japanese ship. Just before the sun came up, a group of planes were approaching from the south about 500 feet above the surface of the ocean. I noticed that they had their running lights on. There were three planes in the group and looked like Navy SOC biplanes with floats for landing gear. Just for fun as they passed by me at almost eye level, I trained my gun on them and tracked them until they were well past me. They were flying about 500 yards off shore, in line with each other about 600 feet above the sea, I thought if they were Japanese planes I might have been able to hit one as they were only going about 100 mph. I realized they were US Navy patrol planes just coming back from a sweep around the Island. I kept watching them as they passed by Waikiki beach when all of a sudden someone in the location of Fort Derussy started firing what looked like a 30 cal. machine gun with tracers about every fifth round. They arced up into the sky right at the three scout planes. This started a whole barrage of gun fire from all the bases around Pearl Harbor, Hickham Field as well as anti-aircraft fire from all around the area. I suppose every itchy trigger finger in the Islands was waiting to fire at something and this was it! It was later confirmed that all three planes were shot down. I'm not sure about the pilots but I think they all managed to survive the friendly fire. I also heard, later on, from one Coast Guard skipper whose ship was near Hilo, Hawaii, that they saw the gun fire from their post and thought it was another bombing raid. With all that fire power exploding in the sky, I wondered where all the debris landed? I was glad to see the sun come up, even though Diamond Head blocked it directly from us, be cause I was getting tired of this job and wondered what was going to happen this day of December 8th, 1941. It was about 8 AM and I was told to forget guard duty and come in for breakfast. A funny thing about the whole guard duty was that I didn't feel physically tired, I guess that the realization that we were in a big war kept me hyped up.

Chapter 8.

New Duty!

After breakfast I was told to pack a tooth brush and shaving kit and a change of clothes because I had been called up for temporary duty on my old light house buoy tender the Kukui. The orders were to go down to Pier 4 and catch the Kukui's motor launch as she was standing offshore just out side the harbor waiting for me to board her. The ship had orders to put out all the automatic lights around the Islands, this included channel buoy lights. They were short handed in the radio department, so the brass figured, since I had some experience on board this ship it was only logical that I should be the one to go. My thoughts on this new duty weren't very good. First of all, I didn't relish the idea of going to sea in an undergunned and not too swift ship, especially when I knew that the whole Japanese Navy was sitting over the horizon waiting for the proper time to invade the Islands! Anyway, I grabbed a few things, like my cartoons of smokes, cause I knew that they would vanish if I left them in our quarters. We didn't have any lockers for my possessions, as we really didn't need them because everyone was as honest as could be so we never worried about leaving money or anything on our beds. It would be there when you came back but since I was leaving on an unknown adventure, with the possibility of not returning, I figured I'd better take my smokes with me. As I was stepping out of the back door to board the old panel truck for the trip down to Honolulu Harbor, I said a few good byes to all the guys in the kitchen and left with the feeling that I would never come back from this mission. The whole group looked at me as if I were going to be executed or walk the plank or hike the thirteen steps to the gallows. I could see it in the eyes of everyone as I left. It really was like going into the unknown since we didn't know where or how many Japanese ships were around us. It was a very scary time, since we hadn't heard any news about what was going on. We did hear several different versions of the casualties list, from around 400 to around 5000 killed or wounded. There was no word on where the Japanese Navy was! With those thoughts in my head I tried to not show any anxiety over what was going on around me. I was driven down to pier 4 and caught the motor launch which was waiting for me. The ship was laying offshore out side of the harbor entrance. The executive officer, Warrant Bosun Anderson, was sitting in the launch waiting for me. On the way out to the Kukui he filled me in on what we were going to be doing. We were going to the North West section of the Islands first. Then work back to Oahu putting out every automatic light as quickly as possible. He then told me that he was going to have to make a difficult decision on an important and tragic situation he had been given while down town at the district headquarters. He was told that one of the engineering crew member's wives had been killed by a Japanese's bomb while she was coming out of their church which was located in the Kimaki district of Honolulu. Knowing that we had to sail immediately and we couldn't spare anyone from this assignment he wondered if he should tell this crew member or just not say anything until we got back to home base. He then said, "He was afraid that the crew member might do something drastic if he found out while we were still near the harbor." He looked at me as if I could give him a clue as how to handle this situation, but I didn't respond because if I gave the wrong answer it might backfire in me, since I was only a third class radioman. When we boarded the ship and boarded they set sail immediately in the direction of the island of Kauai. I don't know whether the executive officer ever told the crew member of his misfortune during this trip.

Being a buoy tender work ship, the Kukui didn't have any real armament. All the arms on board were a dozen or so Springfield 30:06 caliber rifles and a few automatic pistols like the 1911 45 caliber Colt which was the regular GI issue. The ship was painted in the traditional colors of the old light house service, a black hull and a white super structure with beige painted booms and working gear. She had a large boom on her forward work deck that was used for lifting or picking up channel buoys that could weigh around 15 tons or better, including the added weight of the heavy anchors attached to them. The ships power plant was steam which was made by two Scotch boilers that generated the power for the two triple expansion engines that drove the twin screws, plus steam power to the donkey engine up forward on the bow and all the auxiliary gear such as the large boom for hoisting buoys out of the water and driving the electrical generators, which were direct current. The ship was fairly old I think she was built during the first world war or close to it. After boarding the vessel, I stowed what little gear I had brought in the radio shack, which was also my working area and my living quarters. I greeted the radio man, who had relieved me when I was transferred to Diamond Head. The first thing we did was set up a watch schedule between us. He decided to take the first watch which was just a loud speaker monitoring watch in case there was a call for us, since we were in radio silence mode for ships, it was impotant to keep our ears open for any signal for us. As soon as the motor boat was hoisted aboard we headed in the direction of Kauai the Northern most Island. By this time we were going past Hickham field so I went out side to see what kind of damage the bombing had down. We were about where the John Rogers airport was located when I spotted what I thought was a P40 air corps plane lying on the beach just beyond the breakers. Later on I was told that it was a SBD 2 man Navy bomber that had flown in from the Enterprise, one of our main aircraft carriers and got caught without any ammo to fight with as they were just coming in to land at Ford Island. I think, as this was a routine practice when a carrier was coming in from maneuvers. One of the men on the plane had been wounded, there was no word on what happened to the other crew member. I find out at this time that in the book "THE BIG E," It reads: "Ensign E.T. Deacon, piloting an SBD a member of Scouting Six off the Enterprise, used up all his ammunition in a hopeless dogfight with the murderous Zeros and then with a wounded leg and a shot-up aircraft, he glided for Hickham Field. It was just a little too far and he landed in the water just short of the runway, unpacked and inflated his rubber boat, lifted his wounded gunner aboard and paddled ashore. When he was certain that the gunner was in good hands, he some how got through the burning madhouse of Pearl Harbor and across to Ford Island." Toward Hickham Field I could see many damaged planes and hangers with large jagged holes with lots of smoke drifting and swirling around. As we passed the entrance to Pearl Harbor, I could see ships lying around in canted positions and everything looked like it was in disarray. It looked as if we were vulnerable for more attacks. I suddenly realized, that here we were going into the unknown, having no idea where the Japanese fleet was and us with no armament to fight with. About four hours out of Honolulu we were being looked over by an Army Air force bomber. The bomber looked like an A20A, a twin engine plane with radial engines. It was one of the earlier production bombers stationed in the Hawaiian area. It circled over us at a very low altitude about two or three times making everyone on board very nervous. Remember, this was only 24 hours or so after the sneak attack and we didn't' look like any US Military vessel. They may have thought that we were a Japanese ship trying to sneak into the area. I even looked up at the foremast to see if we were flying the ensign, (our flag) it looked like it was . kind of small and I was hoping that they could see it while they were circling us. They finally left us alone and continued on their patrol much to our relief.

While passing between Kauai and Niihau on our way to the automatic light on Lehua Rock we spotted a life boat being rowed across the channel. They looked like they were headed for Kauai. We counted six men rowing this craft. Our chief quarter master suggested to the captain that we should pick up this group in the life boat but the skipper said I don't think that they are in that much trouble. Our priority is to put out all the automatic lights so that the Japanese can't use them to zero in on Pearl Harbor at night. The quarter master said, "Our prime mission in the CG was to rescue seamen in trouble." The captain said, "This is true but we are in a war now and we also in the Navy," so, "We will continue on our way to Lehua Rock.

We arrived at Lehua Rock in the afternoon and found that we couldn't dock our work boat at the landing due to the rough waters. Someone suggested that if we couldn't climb up to the top of the rock to put out the lights, that maybe we could shoot them out with some tracer bullets from our Springfield 30:06 rifles. The captain thought that would be a good idea so we broke out a box of rifles that had been stored and packed in cosmoline (a rust preventive grease) and gave them to those who were going to be shooting at the shed holding the gas containers, first they had to clean the rifles, to get rid of the preservative so they would function properly. After cleaning a few rifles we started shooting tracers at the housing that contained the gas bottles. Soon the shed started burning and the whole thing went up in flames and burned to the ground. We were very sure that there would be no light at this point until we came back to repair the damage after the war's end. We started back to Port Allen, on Kauai. On the way we copied a message that a Japanese submarine had been sighted from shore on the eastern side of the Island. This made the whole crew very nervous. We were running as fast as we could go, which was about 12 knots, without running lights showing and the night was pitch black. We were trying to get to Port Allen without running into any enemy submarines. We were steaming along blindly when all of a sudden the ship shuddered and groaned, then bounced and bounced around coming to a screeching halt! We had run aground! I jumped out of my chair and ran out on deck to see if I could see anything. Much to my surprise I could see coconut palm tree branches almost touching me, they seemed to be very close to the side of the ship. About that the time the executive officer, who is second in command, came running up to me and said, "Get on the radio and send an SOS." I thought to myself that, "We don't send SOS'S in the Coast Guard," I replied to the executive officer, "I can't send that message unless it is authorized by the captain and it is written by him." I don't know if this was the case but it stopped him cold and he turned around and grunted something unintelligible and ran back to the bridge. He didn't come back so I began to gather all-important things that I should salvage like my five cartons of Camels and my Zippo lighter, oh yes an our strip cipher board (secret word code machine), a very important item, some thing that the enemy would like to find. As I stepped out on deck I noticed that the old light house gang were trying to launch the lifeboat and were having trouble getting it out over the water. I was busy putting on my life jacket although it seemed as if we could probably walk ashore. Then I noticed that the captain was rocking the ship by working the twin screws back and forth from reverse to forward motion like you would work an auto stuck in the mud or snow.

After several long minutes we broke free from that coral patch and floated free. We then steamed blindly towards Port Allen, well away from the shore line of the Island. The work crew put the life boat back into its cradle land I put my cartons of Camel's back in my carrying bag and placed the strip cipher back in its proper place. The engineers and the bosun mate checked the hull for any leaks and found no dangerous looking breaks or holes, everything looked OK. We arrived at Port Allen early in the morning at started work on putting out the channel buoy lights. About midmorning a contingent of Army brass came aboard to see the captain. There was a conference going on amongst the Army brass and our officers. We soon found out that we were going to go on a rescue mission and that we would be taking some army personnel with us. I soon found out what the mission was all about.

Chapter 9.

Rescue Mission!!

It seems that a Japanese fighter plane had crashed on Niihau and the pilot had taken control of the island. I guess officially this was the first territory that the Japanese had captured from the USA. While waiting for the Army personnel to come aboard we started to put out the navigation lights around the harbor. The first thing we tried was an attempt at making the job easy by shooting out the lights on the channel buoys like we had done at Lahua Rock. Much to our chagrin the lenses on the buoys were so tough that a 45 cal. bullet wouldn't even put a nick in the glass, we had to board each buoy and shut down the gas supply, which made it a time consuming job. The army group finally came aboard late in the afternoon. We weighed anchor and we were on our way to recapture the Island of Niihau! While on the way over, the Army men and a few of our crew made up a rescue team to recapture the Island. My radio partner who was an ex marine volunteered to go with the raiding party and was accepted. I was glad to stay on board the ship as I felt this could become a very dangerous mission and some one had to monitor the radio signals in case there was a message for us. It was dark when we arrived offshore of Niihau. We had the group of Hawaiians that had rowed over to Kauai to inform the Army about the downed plane and the pilot's holding everyone captive, so we used them to guide us to a safe landing on the Island. Before I go on, here is a little bit of history about Niihau, as told to me. The Robertson Brothers owned the Island and they didn't allow anyone but native Hawaiians to live on the island with a few exceptions, that exception was a Japanese servant who took care of the Robertson house and another Japanese worker who was a bee keeper and of course the Robertson family. These two servants were forced to side in with the Japanese pilot and help him keep the Hawaiians captive. The pilot had convinced the servants that the Japanese had taken over control of all the Hawaiian Islands and they had better help him or face dire consequences. The pilot was armed with a service revolver and the synchronized machine gun which he had removed from its mount off the wrecked plane. This machine gun was the type that fired through the propeller. Why he had it was a mystery because it could not be used as a machine gun out side of its gun mount on the plane. I doubt that the Hawaiians had any fire arms to combat this captor. I learned later that there was a shot gun or two kept on the island.

After a long silent wait on board ship, the landing party returned with the news that the Japanese pilot had been killed by one of the Hawaiians! This Hawaiian was about 6 foot six and weighed at least 275 lbs, a well built and strong man. The Hawaiian charged the pilot as the pilot started shooting him, after receiving three shots in the groin he grabbed the pilot in the middle and tilted him upside down, smashing him hard into the ground killing him instantly. Then his wife proceeded to slice off both of both of the pilots ears, for good measure! Most of the raiders assembled in the radio shack which was quite large and displayed all the items that the pilot had used to control the Island, such as the synchronized machine gun and its ammunition belt full of 7.7 mm bullets. They also found a water proof oil skin belt packet wrapped around his waist that contained a Honolulu High school student body card from Mckinley high school, a map of Oahu, and various items that would help him if he had crashed on Oahu. The landing party left the pilot's body for the locals to bury figuring that the ID documents they found would be good enough for the intelligence branch. We found out that the Army was a bit unhappy about leaving the body over on Niihau. The big Hawaiian walked off the ship to the ambulance after refusing to be carried off the ship on a stretcher. This was the first Island recaptured during WW2.

Chapter 10.

Pear Harbor!

After extinguishing all the automatic lights in the Kauai Island area, we headed back to Oahu. We were immediately sent to Pearl Harbor to mark all the sunken ships and hazards with marker buoys. We came down the main channel past the big dry docks, circled around Ford Island, past the Utah and back to the Ten Ten docks surveying what needed to be done. What a tragic sight to see, debris, oil, overturned ships, sunken battleships sitting on the bottom with some of their gun turrets under water, damaged cruisers, auxiliary ships and supply ships, all showing signs of bomb damage. Most of the Navy's PBY'S, (the twin engine flying boats), were destroyed while parked on Ford Island, the buildings were burned and bombed out. My first impression upon seeing the battleship Arizona was like looking at a distorted picture on film that had been exposed too much heat and had started to melt. I couldn't believe that so much damage could be done to our Navy it was very unreal to me. When we circled Ford Island, I saw the old Utah was completely upside down. I guess the Japs thought they had destroyed an aircraft carrier, it was only a target ship for the dive bombers to practice bombing her at sea, she had a deck of heavy planks which gave her the look of a carrier. Going around again near the dry docks, I could see that the ships in one of dry docks were hit very bad, the Pennsylvania being one of the many causalities in the dry docks. The Ogalala was lying on her side and the destroyer Shaw had its bow blown off almost all the way to the bridge, she was in dry dock number two with the Pennsylvania. In the distance we could see what the bombs and strafing did to Hickham Field. Their hangers were full of gaping holes, roofs were caved in and there were wrecked planes strewn all over the field. You may wonder how I got to see all of this but if you remember I mentioned that we could stand a loud speaker watch, so I stood outside the radio shack with the door open and the receiver turned up loud enough for me to hear any call for our ship. I wished that I had a chance to take some pictures but we were never allowed to take pictures in Pearl Harbor because it was a restricted area, we never attempted to take any but I wondered how many pictures were taken of the area from the hills above Pearl Harbor.

We could see that we had our work cut out for us. The skipper decided to launch the work boat the way that the Cutters did while going under way. We were traveling about two or three knots while we attempted this launch. The work crew was composed of ex-Light House civil service personnel who had not had any training in this procedure. As the boat hit the water, the bowman released his hook first so that the boat swung around and was being dragged along side the ship running backwards. It started banging against the side of the ship. The captain seeing the predicament the boat crew was in, rang for slow astern to stop our forward motion, meantime the seaman on the stern hook was fighting hard to release that hook from the eyebolt but wasn't having much luck releasing it. The seaman handling the after davit line was trying to pay out the falls so that he could get a chance to release the hook from the stern eye bolt, there was too much pressure on it with the ship in motion. He finally broke the hook loose just as the end of the falls were about to unravel, (The davits are the structure that holds the block and tackle that makes it possible to swing the boat over the water and lower it away, the hooks are insert into the eye bolts fasten on the boats bow and stern), Everyone breathed a sigh of relief, it was a close call and the skipper never tried that one again. It made us look unskilled working in the harbor. To do that type of a launch properly there should have been a sea painter attached to the bow of the work boat with an easy slip knot type for release, such as a bowline pin shoved through a loop, then the other end of the sea painter was attached close to the bow so as to give the crew plenty of room to move away from the ship they before release the sea painter. This should keep the whale boat headed in the right direction.

We finished our work and left Pearl Harbor before dark and returned to Pier Four. I noticed that engineers had put up net barricades at both Pearl Harbor and Honolulu entrances during my time at NMO. When we arrived at the dock, several officers were standing by with messages and instructions for some of us. We had hardly gotten tied up when an officer from the district office came looking for me. What he wanted to know why I hadn't contacted my folks yet? His question made me very irritated, so being a radioman I replied by asking him, "How could I possibly contact them while at sea all this time and we were observing radio silence?" He avoided answering my question and said that my folks had been sending telegrams about my welfare almost every day. I wondered why the district office hadn't answered that simple request but I didn't ask why they hadn't, being just a lowly petty officer. It must have been the uncertain where abouts of the enemy and that we may never get back from our assignment. We learned later that there were about six or eight large subs hanging around Pearl Harbor trying to retrieve their two man subs that they had launched just before the bombing raid. One of the subs, I-170, was sunk near the French Frigate Shoals by an Army Air Corp bomber two weeks after the raid. The French Frigate Shoals is just North of the Hawaiian Islands.

After we finished tying up and putting the radio room at rest, I requested permission to leave the ship and go down town to the Western Union office where I could send a short message to my folks saying that every thing was OK and not to worry, I would write to them soon. Thinking that if I sent that message to my father's office in San Francisco, California, they would get the word sooner. So I addressed it to the Pacific Shipowners

Ass. Which caused great laughter in the telegraph office as the clerk corrected the Ass to Assoc.

When I returned to the ship still feeling a little foolish for my spelling abbreviation. Since nothing was happening I sat down in the radio shack and played around with the receiver monitor on the emergency commercial band to see if I could pick up any activity from that source even though we were not officially on watch. With the receiver on the loud speaker system I could listen in with out confining myself to the chair, I could wander around the room or lie down in my bunk and just listen. After a few minutes I heard a rough rasping noise which sounded as if the signal was slightly off frequency. I reached over and tried tuning the signal in without success. The signal was very broad and could be received on both sides of 500 kcs. Being curious I called our shore station NMO the station I recently left and asked them if they were hearing this strange signal, they answered yes they were hearing it. Whoever was sending this signal had a very nervous fist the signal sounded like an early spark transmitter which was illegal in all of the modern world. We finally identified the sender it was a poor old Greek tramp steamer wanting to know what was going on and could he put into port in Honolulu? He was having a difficult time communicating and was trying to get his message across through the use of the International Que system agreed upon at the Cairo communication convention in the late 20's or early 30's. This system was set up so that all ships could communicate their intentions in any port in the world or between ships at sea or from ship to any shore station. We heard that the Greek tramp steamer had just missed running into the Japanese task force that had come to bomb Pearl Harbor. I could just imagine what that poor skipper was thinking when he discovered he was in the middle of a big war between Japan and the United States of American. He probably heard about this conflict by listening to the commercial radio broadcasts and his radio operator more then likely picked up lots of our radio messages during that first day of the conflict even though he probably understood very little English. He probably got enough information so that he wanted to come into Honolulu, even though he had no permit or visa to do so. I didn't follow up on his predicament but hoped That he made it back to his home port.

Chapter 11.

A New Assignment.

Late that evening my friend Scott from the CGC Tiger came on board to visit me. The Tiger was tied up at pier Four. We talked about the surprise attack and what each of us had done so far. He told me that they were cruising on patrol near Hickham Field when the bombing started. He said that a bomber was flying past them not too far away, about fifty feet above the water and started shooting at them from the observers seat of the bomber. He said, "I could have hit that plane with a potato, it was so close." I told him about identifying the three bombers as Army planes that fly by me. Before he left he told me that he really wanted to tell me about the opening on the Tiger fot a radioman and asked me If I wanted the assignment? I informed him that I would like to come on board the Tiger as the Kukui wasn't my idea of a fighting ship. I asked him when the transfer could be made if they accepted me and he said I should get the transfer immediately so put in your request. So I submitted my request to the district office for a transfer to the CGC TIGER a 125-foot patrol boat.

Chapter 12.

The New Assignment.

The Tiger was built by Brown-Boveral in Camden, New Jersey, for the price of $63,173:00. She was commissioned on May 23, 1927 and decommissioned on August 21, 1947. The Tiger was 125 feet long and displaced at about 450 tons. Her hull was riveted and she had wooden decks over steel plates. She was driven by two diesels, either Cooper Bessimers or Winston engines to her twin screws and she had a 32-volt DC battery powered electrical system that powered the radio shack and all other electrical requirements. Every thing on board was pretty basic. She didn't have refrigeration, except ice type storage, she had air cooled storage lockers top side for fresh fruit and vegetables like cabbage and potatoes. The navigation guidance system was a large magnetic compass on the bridge by the wheel with repeater cards placed on each wing of the bridge that were adjusted by hand when called out by the navigator in the wheel house. They were primarily used with a polaris instrument to check our position by sighting land markers as shown on navigational charts. In the radio shack there were a low frequency transmitter and a high frequency transmitter with receivers to match. There was an RDF, radio direction finder, for locating ships in trouble by zeroing in on their signals when detected. There was a newly installed submarine detection device called sonar, built by the Boston Submarine Signal

Corporation, this devise could listen under water and could also send a signal out to detect an object under water and tell you how far away it was from the ship, similar to a depth finder but more sophisticated. In conjunction with this sonar gear were ten depth charge drums weighing 450 lbs each, mounted on two racks hanging over the stern of the ship, one on the starboard side and one on the port side. The racks held 5 drums each. The control gear for dropping the depth charges was up in the wheel house and was a hydraulic motivated system. She had a 3-inch 23 single action manual controlled cannon that was placed forward of the bridge on the main deck which was originally used to fire warning shots across the bow of any ship that refused to stop when ordered to. There were two Lewis 30 caliber machine guns that could be mounted on each wing of the bridge. The rest of the armor was Springfield rifles and automatic 45 Colt hand guns. They built these cutters primarily for prevention of smuggling liquor or drugs to our shores. The crews living quarters were in the forward section of the ship below the main deck. The chief petty officers shared this space also. The officers had their quarters amidships on the starboard side below the main deck. On the port side opposite the officer's stateroom was the location of the galley and all the necessary things connected to feeding the officers and crew. Just aft of the galley were the crews mess deck which took up the whole width of the ship. This was also our hangout, many games of poker or black jack were played here during our time off. In back of the mess deck was the lazaret which was sealed off from the mess deck making it a water proof compartment. The entrance to this compartment was top side on the main deck through a hatch that was normally dogged,(locked), down. Once we tried to drill a hole in the steel plate separating the mess deck from the lazaret locker and found out that the bulk head was made out of armor plating. We almost broke a few arms when the drill caught in the partially drilled hole which threw the drill machine around instead of the bit. Later we were informed that it was against naval regulations to drill into a water proof compartment. The lazaret locker was where all the tow lines and extra gear like fire axes and such, were stowed and just below that was where the rudder yoke for steering the ship was located. The steering mechanism was a mechanical cable assembly. Because of this, the helmsmen were all warned about the dangers of handling the steering wheel when going astern since it was a mechanical cable assembly. There was terrific pressure on the wheel and if you lost your grip or couldn't hold it, the wheel would begin to spin around very fast so that you couldn't grab the spokes to stop the spin. The inherent danger in trying to stop the wheel by grabbing the spokes was that it could break your arm or hand. It was best to let it go to the stops at the end of its turn. The ship was designed to make long range cruises without refueling. Cruising for 10,000 miles was possible before it needed to be refueled. The only trouble was the food got to be the problem, especially fresh food and milk.

Chapter 13.

The Tiger Maru!

My transfer came in immediately. All I had to do was go out to the station at NMO and pick up all my belongings. The skipper, Chief Warrant Mazzoni gave me permission to go out and get everything in my own auto the Studebaker Rockne that Scott and I owned. While collecting everything I talked to the chief and he told me that all our logs for the 6th and the 7th of December were sent to the Roberts Congressional Report for scrutiny. I loaded up everything I had into the old Stude, said farewell to the gang and drove back to the Tiger in time for evening chow.

Since we were now in a war and uncertain as to where we would be going, Scott and I decided we should sell the car as soon as possible. A first class cook, in rating only not by endeavor, stationed on board the ship decided to buy the car because he lived on the Island with his wife and they could use the car. Needless to say we sold it pretty cheap to him. Scott closed the deal for us. The cook decided to start a laundry service for the ship using his wife as the person who would do the laundry at their house for a fairly good rate. There were no laundry facilities on board the ship. Everyone on board had to do his laundry by hand out of a bucket or in a wash basin. The cook's enterprise ended rather abruptly when several lively scorpions were found in the fresh laundry. Apparently they hung the clothes on lines berneath part of the house. They build many houses in Hawaii rather high on stilts so that the area could be used for parties or drying clothes or whatever. There must have been lots of scorpions in his basement area to find two or three scorpions in the clothes hanging out to dry.

Just after he lost the laundry contract he decided to test his driving ability after a good drinking binge and failed miserably as he ended up smashing the poor old Rockne into a large coconut tree somewhere in the Kimiki district on his way home. He was slightly injured and the Rockne ended up in the junk pile.

We moved the Tiger down near the Aloha Tower because it was getting too crowded at Pier Four. This didn't go over too well with the crew because it placed us away from our favorite watering holes. Across the street from Pier 4 was the Naval dispensary or first aid station and down the street a little further on the same side was bar restaurant by the name of Maggie's Inn and around the corner from there was funny little bar with a dirt floor called Kakioki Inn which served beer and wine only. Going to Maggie's Inn in the morning for a cup of coffee was fun. There was a Japanese waitress that used to call me, "swede, my wadioman" which brought gales of laughter from all the gang. The dispensary ran movies at night which we could attend whenever we wanted to go while in port. I will never forget the first time we went over there during a total black night with no moon shining down on us, it must have been about five or six days after the 7th, you couldn't see a thing, not even your hand in front of your face, as we started across the street the guard yelled HALT! Who goes there? Boy did we halt fast! "Advance and be recognized," he said in a loud voice. We answered USCG real quick and very loudly. I think he was pointing that loaded rifle directly at us. Though we couldn't see him on this very dark night, it felt as if he really was pointing that rifle at us. We were pretty darn nervous and wondered if it was worth getting shot at just to see a movie. We were aware of shooting going on every night because we could see gun shot flashes all over this side of the Island while we were on patrol between Diamond Head and Barber's Point. It paid to be cautious when approaching any military guard position at night. They told me later that some guards would fire their machine guns testing them to make sure they were working properly. How true that was I'm not sure.

While we were tied up near the Aloha Tower location, our communication officer, H.M. Anthony, came down from the district office to the ship on some errand and while there spoke to me about coming up to the office for an interview. So I went directly to his office as soon as possible. When I got there, he said hello and asked me if I could copy

20 words a minute. Of course the answer was yes. He then said, "Congratulations you are now a 2nd class radioman!" I was amazed because I expected to take some sort of written test for that rating and I had been studying quite a bit so that I would be ready whenever they decided to give me the test. He had put me up for this rating a couple of months before and I didn't pass the material part of it verbally because I never had any schooling on electronics and the warrant officer who gave me the test was a sticker for the electronic's part, which irritated H.M. Anthony very much because he wanted me to have that RM2C rating. Another thing that may have helped my promotion was the fact that we were in a war on two fronts, Europe and the Pacific.

On this ship they gave me a lower bunk in the forecastle where all the enlisted men were quartered. While putting away all my belongings in my locker in a ship shape manner I began to think of what my duties would be like. One thing that I noticed was the new wire cage that was placed in the middle of our quarters. It was located right against the water proof bulkhead and protruded about 4 feet into our space. The cage contained the shaft, hydraulic system and the sonar ball that were located under the keel and was built so that it could be lowered below the keel about 2 feet and used to detect submarines. The electronic part of the sonar equipment was located on the bridge just behind the helm against the bulk head that housed the radio equipment. They had installed this sonar gear a few months previously and it was our main offensive weapon to be used in tracking down enemy submarines. The device was made by the Boston Submarine Signal Company, a company that made such things as depth sounders and underwater listening devices. I figured that I should learn about this gear because it paid extra money if you qualified as a specialist in sonar operating.

One of my other duties beside being a radio operator was correcting the aids to navigation book. This book was kept at the chart desk where they plotted our navigation courses. The reason we were given that duty, was because we had no quartermaster ratings on the ship and all the notices came by radio. These notices were for world wide navigation and we would paste the notice over the old navigation aid printed in the book. Some times we would just red line an aid that was eliminated. There were many such changes like new channel markers or a change in light sequence in a channel buoy or a marker for a hazard to navigation. We also got restricted notices on some naval encounters with enemy ships or submarines and were given information on the tactics used to evade or fight off forces if it was plausible. One such notice described the action of a squadron of four stack destroyers running into a large contingent of Japanese heavy cruisers and many destroyers where they would have been soundly defeated. It described the action thusly, "we saw a huge fog bank ahead and used it to hide from the Japanese force." They passed through the whole convoy of enemy ships in the fog bank and when they were challenged by blinker light code they would send back gibberish signals, which the Japanese signalmen eccepted, mainly because they didn't want their superior officers to know they couldn't read what was being sent." In this way they passed through the whole enemy convoy and made their escape to safety. This information on action with enemy forces was restricted information, not to be read by everyone on the ship. Also, the aids to navigation notices were handled by a quartermaster and since we didn't have a quartermaster rating or even a signalman on board this type of vessel, it was dumped on the radiomen. Since we knew morse code real good, we got the job of being signal man too.

Chapter 14.

On Patrol!

On one of my first patrols on the Tiger we heard that the small Army transport that traveled between the Islands had just been torpedoed in the Molokai Channel and had sunk. We were just passing through the submarine net that stretched across the entrance to Honolulu Harbor, so we knew that there was plenty of danger out there at sea. Our patrol which covered the area from Barbers Point to Diamond Head buoy, was uneventful and we returned to the base in Honolulu after a seven-day patrol. While we were in port, we heard a rumor that the Reliance, our sister ship had spotted a periscope near the harbor entrance and that the skipper refused to do any thing about it. I don't know how true this was but the crew was very upset about not taking any action on this sighting. We heard that the skipper was relieved of his command after that.

With our total blackout being observed the volcano on Mt Mauna Loa began erupting and lighting up the sky at night. We all thought that this would be a tough light to put out. It sure gave the enemy a line as to where the Island was but I don't think it really gave them any help as far as pinpointing any target to shell on shore. The eruption lasted about three days and then she went back to sleep for quite a while much to our relief. We would have had a rough time if we had to evacuate the whole island of Hawaii during this crisis with all those Japanese submarines roaming around. On our very next patrol, Jenkins our senior radioman and sonar operator, made contact with a definite pinging response. It appeared that a Japanese sub was lurking around the area just off Kewalo Yacht Basin which is near Ft Derussy and Waikiki Beach. We went into a general quarters mode and the tension began building up while we prepared to attack this submarine. Everyone was keyed up as we charged toward the enemy at a top speed of 13 & ½ knots. Both engines were going at their maximum allowed rpm's. When the sonar signal disappeared that meant we were about to pass over the submarine. I had learned this reading the sonar manual. In the meantime the skipper, told the depth charge rack personnel to set the depth charges at 100 feet which meant that they would explode when they reached that depth. Each charge had a primer that had the depth scale indicator setting starting at 100 feet on up to about 300 feet. Later depth chargers had a depth of 75 feet but that was for ships that could move fast enough to get out of the way.

The tension built up as we charged toward our unseen enemy! The skipper yelled, "Stand by to drop number one." Then exclaimed, "Drop it," Then he said, "Stand by to drop number two, drop it," They were both dropped as commanded by way of the hydraulic control levers situated on the bridge and activated by a seaman who was striking for a gunner's mate rating. All this time I was standing on the flying bridge above the wheel house where I could see and hear everything that was happening. When the charges went off I could see how powerful these depth charges were by the way they lifted the ship up a couple of feet high and a huge geyser of water would appear about 20 feet above the sea. It felt as if a giant had taken a huge hammer and hit the bottom of my feet. To continue the attack we quickly came about, got up to speed again and dropped two more depth charges in the same area. We couldn't get a good response out of our sonar equipment because of all the disturbance we had caused when we dropped the charges. We then shut down our engines and drifted around looking for oil slicks or maybe some clothing or even a body just anything to show that we had a Japanese submarine sunk to our credit. Finally a large dazed sea turtle surface about a hundred yards from the ship and slowly swam away looking very tired. Oh yes, there were things, killed like some little colored fish about the size of a small perch but nothing else appeared on the surface. Half the deck crew was standing around with lines tied to buckets ready to scoop anything that resembled parts of a submarine but to no avail. We felt a little embarrassed for not getting a hit. We had visions of being big heroes and would be able to put markers of a Japanese sub on the wings of the bridge or the smoke stack as the destroyers did.

Then the engine room gang began calling the bridge to tell them that they had a problem in the engine room. It seems that when the charges went off it broke several water pipe connections especially wherever there was an elbow connection. My friend Jim, Machinist Mate 2C, said he thought that we would have to go in for repairs right away. Just about then someone recalled that a destroyer had depth charged this area the last time we were on patrol in this area, which was the run between Barbers Point and Diamond Head Buoy.

While in port we found out that the main sewer line from the city of Honolulu ended just about where we were dropping those charges which is about a mile offshore. As far as I was concerned, this was a good lesson on how not to attack a submarine. First, your depth charges should be dropped in sequence right from the beginning of your attack, then after that look for signs of the submarine away from the area where the depth charges were dropped in case you missed it or had just damaged it a little. Also have enough speed running in on the target area so as not to damage your own ship.

After witnessing that action I felt more than ever like getting into the sonar operation as working the radio shack was very boring. Since we entered into the war we were not permitted to transmit any messages, the exception being if you are sinking and there was no other way of getting the information to your command. Then it would be considered an absolute emergency and you could go ahead and send that message! As far as the radio work was concerned, all we did was copy Fox schedule messages. All these messages were encrypted (coded) along with the ships addresses or name so if you didn't have your ships call letters already encrypted for the day you wouldn't know if the message you were copying was for you or not. They made most messages up in five letter groups and there were various types of cryptograph methods used, such as strip cipher, wheel ciphers, etc. All messages had priority classifications from urgent to deferred classes, so I figured that if I could run the sonar gear maybe I could sink a submarine which would be much more satisfying than copying CW messages in Morse code at 20 words a minute. Also the commissioned officers were the only ones who were supposed to work the encoding devices but this never worked out on a small ship. The executive officer thought that I should have the job, so I had the work encoding and decoding messages, mostly decoding as we never sent any messages out.

Getting back to the sonar equipment I found that our sonar hadn't been tried out too much, in fact I think it had a canvas cover over the instrument until that patrol on Dec. 7th. The captain didn't have much faith in what the sonar could do so he never used it until the 7th. Since we were a 32-volt DC electrical system and the sonar required a 110-volt AC system they had to install a diesel powered engine to run a 115 VAC at 60 cycles generator. Jenkins, the RM1C in charge of the radio and sonar gear, gave me a good run down on how the sonar operated. If I got good enough and could qualify as a sonar operator I would get an extra five dollars a month for running sonar. At the time there was no classification or rating for a sonar or radar operator. We sent one radio operator to radar school over at Pearl Harbor and he studied all about radar antenna's, transmission lines and associated equipment. Nevertheless, we never had any of this gear installed on board the whole time I was aboard the Tiger.

While studying the tactics of submarines, we discovered that one of the most important maneuvers to look for was the turn that a submarine would make during its evasive tactics. The reason being that once the submarine committed itself to the turn there wasn't much of a chance for changing course again since the response time for the change was too long to make. We could almost predict the exact spot where the sub would be before it could respond to any change of direction. This enabled us to come very close to a direct hit by dropping our depth charges in a diamond pattern using both the over the stern drop and the firing of the side charges in the proper sequence to lay that effective pattern. The only thing that was discouraging was the fact that we didn't have the side charges to fire and we were poorly equipped for navigating. A magnetic compass, with an 8-inch card, was our only guidance system. The Polaris repeaters on the wings of the bridge were only static placed cards with the compass readings printed on them which you had to adjust according to the magnetic compass in the wheel house, this was done by calling out the readings and then the person sighting through the Polaris sights would adjust his card for a proper reading which meant that the ship could not change or swing off that course until after you got your sighting. Since the sonar gear had a compass card that should have been slaved to a gyrocompass, a repeater card, we had to set the card permanently north using the bow of the ship as our north. If we contacted any sub and the ship changed course we could completely lose contact because we had no way of knowing which way the ship was heading without a true repeating card working in the sonar gear. It was very frustrating to say the least. I started working on the up keep and maintenance of this gear as no one else seemed to want to do it.

By studying the manual I learned how to operate the equipment and how to keep it running smoothly. Down in the crew's quarters where the cage was located I noticed that the work men who had done the installation had never cleaned up the deck around the shaft where it went through the hull, it looked very messy. So I got busy and scraped all the crud off the deck and repainted the steel plating with zinc chromate and then painted over that with a pure white enamel paint so that the area looked clean enough to use for a food bar. When our new skipper came aboard a few months later he was very impressed with the looks of that area which helped my standing with him after that.

We soon got an extra gadget to tie in with the sonar tracking device which would give us a relative reading as to what depth a submarine would be at and what setting should be put on the firing device. This was figured out because of the angle of the ping signal which was such that when we lost the return signal, say at 200 yards we knew from the angle of the signal that the sub would be at a certain depth and it would tell us we should be passing over the spot where the submarine should be. This device would take over the dropping of the charges at the proper depth and time. We never had a chance to use this instrument at sea while I was on board the ship but we did use something like it at the subbase in Pearl Harbor when using their simulation machine to practice our submarine tactics against the crews of submarines like the Argonaut. I will go into detail later because these were exciting days for me.

Chapter 15.

Rescue.

It was on my next patrol that we were told to look for a lifeboat that had been spotted about 200 miles west of the Island by an Army Air Force patrol bomber. We spent the whole day going West when we copied a message from NPM on the Fox sked, that a navy destroyer had found the life boat and had the crew members on board and that they were heading back to Pearl. We then turned around and headed home also. Three or four hours later another message came over the NPM Fox schedule

153

that another patrol bomber had sighted another lifeboat. It was in the same area where they sighted the first lifeboat. We turned around and headed back out toward the west wondering if there was a screw up in communications. We thought we could be on a wild goose chase. Late that afternoon we did spot a lifeboat on the horizon with a small jury rigged sail on her. It took about another hour to reach her and we could see quite a few sailors on board. As we approached them, we could see them hungrily eating chocolate bars that they had been saving for a long journey at sea. We pulled along side the lifeboat, tied it to the ship, and they all began to climb aboard. They were tired, hungry and ragged looking and some of them had facial wounds plus they were all sunburned. After removing all the lifeboat equipment such as the boat compass and very signal pistol, (a pistol that shoots colored flares), we cut the boat loose and let it drift ahead of our ship. We didn't want to tow it back with us and we didn't want to leave drifting around the ocean to be spotted again so the skipper decided to sink it by shooting it with our 30 cal. machine guns. He thought it would be good for a little target practice. We started firing at it putting many holes in the hull. It slowly sank out of sight beneath the surface as we circled it to make sure that it was really gone. After that we immediately started out for Oahu. The captain had the boatswain mate pipe chow call on his bosun pipe and everyone on deck started for the mess deck. Then the skipper, who was standing on the port wing of the bridge, saw what was happening and shouted, "not you guys," meaning the ships personnel whereas the chief mate from the lifeboat crew thought that the skipper meant that they were the group that wasn't supposed to go down to the mess deck. He got very irritated and yelled back so everyone could hear "We don't want any of your lousy chow!" This is when I spoke up and said, "No chief, he meant the ships crew not you people." This calmed him down, we all wanted them to feel welcome as possible, because this is something that we were trained for, saving people at sea. The cook got up a good hot meal for them. There were thirteen men in the life boat and they had been at sea in the boat for thirteen days, I guess that was their lucky number. Most of the survivors were from the engine room and the stewards department with the only deck member being the chief-mate. He had decided to use the sail in order to reach the Hawaiian Islands but since they didn't have a keel on the life boat, the boat kept slipping sideways thus preventing them from getting closer to their goal, the Hawaiian Islands. After they finished eating, we started talking to them about their ordeal. We found out that they were sunk approximately 400 miles south of the Hawaiian

Islands and the name of the ship was the (SS PRUSA) or (SS Parada) out of New York. She had a load of zinc chromate ore in her holds and she was heading for New York via the Panama Canal. They didn't know anything about the attack on Pearl Harbor as they were sunk on the sixth of December. I guess the Japanese forgot about the change in time when they crossed over the International date line.

They told us the story of how they were torpedoed. The submarine was a large vessel, probably an I class sub like the ones that carried the two man subs. It attacked them late at night on December 6th. In the darkness they thought they could see a large deck gun. They said that the sub had fired a few shots at them from that deck gun after they were torpedoed. They even turned on a large search light on them when they were firing this deck gun at them. Because of the load of zinc chromate the ship was going down very fast, in fact it was sinking so fast that their life boat they were in sailed across the deck of the ship as it was sinking, missing all the rigging structures such as the booms and other structures that might have snagged them. The reason that they sailed across the entire deck was that their assigned lifeboat was on the windward side of the ship. They couldn't push away from the hull because of a strong wind which kept pushing them into the hull so they had no choice but to try and go across the deck to the lee side of the ship to get away from her as she sank. As they were crossing the deck, they saw the radio operator running to the radio shack for a try at sending an SOS and to give the position of the ship. The deck officers and deck crew were assigned to the lifeboat that happened to be on the lee side of the ship so they had a pretty easy time of getting clear of the rapidly sinking ship. As I said the chief mate decided to try for the Hawaiian Islands, he didn't see the other lifeboat so he didn't know if they made it off the ship. We told them about the other lifeboat being rescued and we all figured that must have been the one he meant. We found out later that it was not the other crew that was picked up. They were from another ship.

According to an article or story in the Life Magazine, the Captain and the navigator decided to sail westward with the wind. According to the article they spent 21 days in that open lifeboat before they reached a small island which the Japanese held according to the article. This was an article that we all read about three or four months later. It described their ordeal as being such a successful navigating feat that we couldn't help laughing over this story when we realized that these were the deck officers and crew from the same ship that the chief mate and his black gang (Engine room sailors) and steward crews were from. Also after having sailed through dangerous waters, they ended up dodging the Japanese when they did hit shore before being rescued. Thanks to the chief mate the black gang and steward's department took only thirteen days by sailing toward the Hawaiian Isles and they would have been closer to the islands if the life boat had a decent keel to keep the boat sailing in a straight line instead of drifting sideways as they progressed. When we sighted them, they were about 200 miles west of Kauai and they were sailing slowly toward the French Frigate Shoals and Midway Island. I talked to the youngest member of the crew. He said he was eighteen years old, he looked younger than that, and that they signed him on as an oiler in the engine room. He had a very bad cut across his upper lip, it was rather a jagged cut that he had gotten when he crawled through the holes in the decks that the torpedo blast had caused. I don't see how he made it up through those jagged holes, especially after absorbing the shock waves from the torpedo hit. The young oiler told me he wouldn't have made it to the life boat if he hadn't been able to crawl through those spaces. We all marveled at the way these merchant mariners had come through this harrowing experience in such good spirits. We pulled into Honolulu Harbor, tied up at pier four and bid the rescued sailors good bye and good luck. We all felt pretty good about that rescue job.

Chapter 16.
Night Rations.

While tied up at pier four, Scott and I made a run up town to buy groceries for midnight rations. We had to buy food that required no refrigeration, so it had to be such items as Campbell soup, pork and beans, canned meats and crackers. This was our second time at buying food for the night watch standers. After buying enough food for a weeks patrol we started walking back to the ship. On the way back we spotted a large hand printed sign hanging on a window of a feed and grain store proclaiming that they had Calo Dog food on sale. As we passed by the sign, we both thought of the same thing at the same time. "Let's do it," I said, knowing that he was thinking we should get it for our hungry buddies. We went into the feed store and asked, how much for the dog food. They said it was two cans for twenty-five cents. We both laughed and said, "OK we want two cans of that Calo Dog food," just to be buying something on sale. Scott said this should be good enough for all those guys who like to wolf down our rations but never give a thought to helping out by chipping in a little money. Those who did contribute to the cause were informed about our idea of giving it to the night crew. The first night on patrol we mixed up a bowl of Calo with mayonnaise and left it on the counter in the galley. Sure enough, the whole bowl of that mixture disappeared by midnight.

The first victims had this to say about our new rations, James A. Lee RM2C, "There are sharks teeth in this stuff and I only eat this shit to please you guys but it taste like hell." Richard Heddy SEA2C, "It tastes like fish and my tongue sticks to the top of my mouth." James Elliot MM2C, "It must be the bread, it tastes moldy, I've got a cold so I can't taste it all that well and its got lumps in the mixture." These quotes were said on January 7th, 1942, then on January 8th, 1942, Raymond Olsen MM1C said "It looks like shit to me in the dark of the galley." Robert Jenkins RM1C said "I have to see this under the light before I eat it." James Elliot said, "This tuna must be cheaper because it's a lot thicker than the other night so don't forget your little black friend." Pete McFarland RM2C said, "Is this stuff for all hands?" Richard Heddy remarked, "What company makes this stuff? "It must be made in a wooden vat cause I found some wood in it."

"Some pickles would improve this immensely." "I feel indebted to you guys for this so next payday I'll buy some pickles!" These quotes were recorded by Ralph C Nash who also classified us providers as, Ralph C. Nash Chief Chef and Mixer, George C. Larsen Head Pantryman, and Scott P Berryman Adviser and Propagandist. Needless to say, we didn't tell anyone about the mixture for about three days. We told them after that but they really didn't believe us, much to our relief. I could just see the whole crew chasing us around the ship with vengeful intent of doing bodily harm. After that session things went back to normal when it came to midnight rations. Elliot even started heating the beans in the engine room. He used a gasoline blow torch to heat the beans up, as the galley stove was always shut down after the evening meal. By the third trip we had the crew helping us pay for the rations. We bought lots of things like mustard and salad spread, to liven up the sandwiches.

Chapter 17.

Dry Dock.

We went into dry dock for our annual bottom cleaning. It was a privately owned floating dry dock located near Pier Four. They cleaned the bottom and replaced the worn zinc plates on the propeller shafts and made sure that the screws were OK. Looking at the hull out of the water in the floating dry dock made me think that our ship sure looked like a fat old duck. The screws looked so small and the fat duck look gave me an understanding as to why we were not such a fast moving ship. In fact, I

167

wondered how we even got close to fourteen knots as our maximum speed. While in this yard there was another ship being worked on that looked like a yacht. Her name was Azurlight and she was a former yacht being converted into a anti-submarine patrol vessel. We didn't get along with any of the crew mainly because they were all in the Naval Reserve. We heard that the skipper of this yacht was the former owner and that he got his Lt. Jg. commission from the Navy Department for donating the yacht to the Navy for the duration. While we were in dry dock we got every thing in shipshape. At night when we didn't have liberty we had some good poker games. One day I ran into an old friend of mine, Bob Byrnes from Mill Valley, my home town. He told me he was working out at Pearl Harbor as a sheet metal worker and that he had a nice cottage out by Waikiki Beach. He told me that he got a transfer from Mare Island and now there was a better pay rate because he was in a war zone. Jim and I stayed overnight at his cottage a couple of times. It was rather nice living away from the ship. We only got to do it during our time in dry dock. It was interesting riding the electric trolley down town in the early morning with all the ship yard workers. After we started our regular patrols again I didn't see him until after the war and that was back in Mill Valley. During this time my buddy Scott was recommended for chief boatswain mate. He was also recommended for officers candidate school. Scott went down to the district office to take his physical which he passed easily. Right after that he took a test to qualify for the mental part for officers candidate school and passed that one too. I was glad to see that he passed everything. After all the repairs were taken care of we returned to Pier Four. Then right after that, Captain Mazzoni got a notice that he was being transferred back to the states. So

we all began to wonder who our new skipper would
be.

Chapter 18.

The New Skipper.

Just as I was getting used to the officers and crew members on the Tiger Maru, as we called her, Captain Mazzoni got transferred to the mainland and a new skipper came aboard. He came on board with a flair, someone said he had carried on a set of golf clubs. His rank was Lt. and physically he was rather short in sature and looked as if he weighed about 150 lbs. if he were dripping wet. The first thing I learned about him was that he didn't have a high regard for any crew member who didn't have an aptitude for seaman ship. If you didn't show at least some interest in seaman ship then he didn't think your other abilities were very good. Luckily I had lots of experience at being a seaman and knew my way around the ship. One of the first things he looked for was someone to repair his torn hand bag. Since it was a canvas bag I volunteered to repair it for him. When I was finished with it he was very impressed with the way I had sewn it using my leather palm and canvas needle. Then I showed him all of my coxcombing and turks heads,(Fancy woven string), that I had woven all around the ship. Explaining to him that I had done this work on the stanchions and hand rails in my spare time while in port and even while we were on patrol. After the skipper got settled in, he decided to take the ship out into Honolulu Harbor to see how she handled. We backed away from Pier 4 and began going slowly toward Ft. Shafter and the harbor entrance. As I had no duties at the time, I stood on the fore deck just under the bridge to watch how the new skipper was handling the ship. I noticed that we were running pretty close to the shore line so I sauntered over to the port railing to see if I could see the bottom of the bay. I remembered that we had anchored our sailboat in this area and I knew it was pretty shallow. Looking down I saw white sand billowing up like a huge cloud which meant we were plowing into a bank of sand. The skipper must have noticed the ship was slowing down so he yelled at the coxswain to go to the bow and take a lead line reading. By this time we were laughing and smirking and trying not to show our reaction as the coxswain tossed the lead line into the water as close to the bow as he could. When the lead weight hit the water it didn't even get past the first marker which was 1 fathom, a depth of 6 feet. The Captian tried backing the ship down but we were stuck fast. I glanced over to Pier 4 and saw that there was a large crowd of people standing at the end of the dock watching our dismal performance. We could see officers and sailors and even a few civilian employees jumping around slapping each other on the back and having a great time over our dilemma. The new skipper was very embarrassed and later on asked me if I knew about the sand bar, I told him that we had anchored our sail boat near that area but that we weren't too sure of the depth where he was heading for. Much to our discomfort, the Reliance, our sister ship, came out there and pulled us off the sand bar. The whole episode took about 4 hours before we got back to the Pier to tie up. The captain didn't get a reprimand for his sloppy navigation mishap but we sure took a big ribbing from the other ship's, enlisted men and officers.

We were all standing on the dock at pier four, officer's and men from about three ships, just shooting the breeze, when a large troop ship came by on her way to a dock further down the harbor. She was painted in war time colors and everyone on the pier started trying to identify her. The captain, who was still trying to save face over his misfortune, leaned over towards me and whispered, "Swede" what's the name of that ship", I whispered, "It's the old Matsonia" which it wasn't. He said it out loud And everyone laughed. I wondered why I put myself in such a position. He never reprimanded me for that gaffe, thank goodness!

Chapter 19.

Escort Duty.

On our next assignment we were told to escort a navy gasoline tanker which we picked up at the entrance of Pearl Harbor. The direction for the course was toward the big island of Hawaii. I happened to be assigned to the sonar gear that morning. As we started to escort the tanker, I noticed that the captain was escorting this ship on the inboard side, which meant that our ping signal could not get past the tanker because of the disturbance of her screws and wake that she left while under way. I had to explain to the skipper that we couldn't use our sonar to the best of our ability because the tanker was blocking our signal and besides that we should be a few hundred yards ahead of her. After getting in the right position the skipper saw that the tanker was trying to get our attention by signaling with her blinker light. The skipper asked me to act as signalman so I got our blinker gun out since we didn't have a regular blinker signal lamp. This hand blinker gun has a long barrel so that it can only be seen directly in front of the gun at the muzzle. There was no side flash to be seen which is good for night signaling. The tanker started telling us it was going to be in control of this convoy and started giving orders just as we were passing Diamond Head. This made our Captain so infuriated that he sent back a blinker message through me. "No way, I'm in command of this convoy." So they started by asking each other for their seniority numbers since they found out that they held the same rank as Lts. After a trip to the ward room, where the skipper kept his records we found out that our captain was the senior man so we took over the command for running the convoy. Again we settled down to running the convoy with me desperately trying to telling the skipper to get ahead and out side of the tanker which he finally did. Now I felt I could run the sonar gear properly with a full sweep for at least 180 degrees ahead of our path we were heading in, especially since we were in the area where that small US Army transport had been torpedoed and sunk. When we came back to the port of Honolulu after that convoy job I tried to requisition a blinker light for us to use but to no avail I was told that there were no 32 volt blinker lamps made. At the time I took that answer on its merits, now I realize that all we had to do was get the instrument and change the lamp socket to accommodate a 32-volt lamp. Being new at all this I asked the skipper if it would be OK to see if the machinist at Pier 4 could make something up that would work with our regular 12-inch search light. He said, "Do whatever you think will work." So I asked the machinist if he could make a blinker mechanism that would work on our regular search light. He said he would try. He did make a fine shutter system out of copper sheeting and it worked well enough for us to use. The first time I used it was while on patrol between Barbers Point and Diamond Head. A two stack destroyer came steaming out of Pearl Harbor and started blinking at us. The OD called me over and asked me to reply to the destroyer. The message started out as they came steaming by us in the opposite direction I got just about half of the message as they disappeared over the horizon. So the OD (Officer of the Deck) said, "Forget it, we can't accept half a message." I was glad because the message was about some poor guy who had missed the ship and the skipper wanted him in irons or given a court marshal. I had the feeling this poor guy was in deep trouble. For all I know he could have been ill or in an accident while ashore. I'm sure he reported into the base at Pearl as there are no places for a service man to hide on Oahu. All I got out of the episode was the fact that the blinker worked OK.

Chapter 20.

Roger B. Taney.

The Taney was one of our largest cutters. She was 327 feet long and displaced a weight of about 2300 tons and cruised at 18 knots, with a top speed of 21 knots. Before the Taney was sent back to Alameda for rearming and upgrading she happened to be on the same Barbers Point to Diamond Head submarine sweep patrol with the Tiger. The Taney, W37, was the first ship I was assigned to when they transferred me to the 14th Naval district in April of 1940.

On this particular patrol I had just turned in for the night, around midnight, when I felt someone shaking me vigorously and whispering GENERAL QUARTERS! I was astounded that I didn't hear the alarm go off. The chief boatswain mate was telling me in a very low voice that we were at General Quarters. Being half asleep I muttered what is the matter with the alarm system? He replied, "There's a Japanese submarine between the Taney and the Tiger and they can't attack the submarine with gun fire because we are exactly on the other side of the submarine in line with anything that they fire." The submarine is on the surface charging it's batteries. As I started out of my bunk I happened to be looking at the ladder that goes top side and watched one of the seaman trying to put on a pillow thinking it was a life jacket. It was one of the funniest sights to see during the war, it had me laughing so hard I forgot to be frightened about the submarine being there.

We all manned our general quarters stations quietly and quickly. The Chief boatswain explained to us that the Taney had spotted the submarine and had reported it to us via the hand held blinker gun. During this time the submarine dove under water realizing that we had seen her even though it was a very dark night. We all began to maneuver around so as to attack her with our depth charges. The Taney apparently had her sonar signal locked on the sub, or so they thought and started a dept charge run. We were going in the opposite direction at that particular time and hadn't picked up any ping return from our sonar when the Taney let loose with a string of charges. Her charges felt and sounded much stronger than any of the charges that we had dropped. I wondered about that and was told that they had gone to the new 600 pound charges that were to be used against the double hulled German submarines. Since the Japanese were their allies it was thought that they could possibly have built some double hulled ships too. We didn't hear any scuttlebutt latter on as to whether they hit the submarine or not. We wondered if the whole exercise was just war nerves and a lot of imagination on the part of the Roger B. Taney. However our Chief said he saw the submarine and he figured if we had rung our alarm this would have been picked up by the submarines listening device as we were that close to them. Evidently they were alerted any way and probably made it out of the area which was what we were there for since this was right near the Pearl Harbor Channel entrance. We later found out that there were at least six or eight of these large I type submarines hanging around Pearl Harbor after the Dec. 7th raid. We think that they were still trying to recover the two man submarines that they had launched during the raid. We did capture some of those two man submarines and at least two were in the harbor at Pearl. I can still see that seaman struggling to put on his pillow for a life jacket as he climbed up the ladder to his station.

Chapter 21.

Feather Merchant Tests.

While in port we were testing merchant seaman in life boat handling. This was a test for handling a life boat during an emergency such as abandoning. ship, If the seaman passed this test he was qualified to make ordinary seaman in the merchant marine, this was one pay step higher than just a seaman.

Since we were giving these test while in port we put the whale boat over the side and had it tied up to the rail while waiting for the seaman to come down and take the test. In the tropics we had awnings stretched out over most of the deck to give us relief from that fierce tropical sun. On this particular day it started raining very hard. It was such a huge tropical downpour that the water was pouring off the awnings as if we were at Niagara Falls. Everyone was dashing to a shelter, when some one noticed that the line tied to the whale boat looked pretty tight. The boatswain ran over and discovered that the whale boat and the motor whale, both of which were tied up in the water, looked as if they were about to go under except for the lines holding them to the ship. Both boats would have sunk if the mooring lines had broken. We frantically started hauling in on the davits to pick them out of the water and let the water drain out of each boat after we pulled the drain plugs. We never left them in the water after that until we were ready to use them.

The new skipper and I got along pretty well when it came to seamanship so he asked me if I would like to give the merchant seamen the life boat test. I accepted the challenge and was delighted to do as I was well versed in the handling of lifeboats. I gave them a rough time on the tests because I knew that if they got into a real bind on a sinking ship they would have to have all the skills possible in that event. All this testing with the feather merchants (Merchant Marine sailors) made the coxswain unhappy because he figured that he should be giving these test but he made too much of it. He did want to show the skipper that he knew his seamanship skills so he could get advanced in his rating to 2C boatswain mate. For a while I considered changing my rating to boatswain mate, even the skipper thought it was a good idea, but I decided not to because I could see that it would be a long drawn out process and I was already a second class radio man with a sonar speciality rating on top of that.   Any how, seventy five percent of the seaman did pass the tests that I gave.

Chapter 22.

Retrofitting.

Willy Larson came back from radar school he had been attending at Pearl. He was full of radar secrets which he was supposed to keep to himself. I don't know what the higher ups were thinking of, maybe that we would be selling these secrets to the enemy. He did give us a few hints on how it worked and how delicate the instrument was. It didn't sound like anything I would be interested in because I was already deep into the workings of sonar. Mean while the scuttlebutt was that we were going into Pearl Harbor for upgrading everything on the ship including some bigger and better anti-aircraft guns. Also they were going to get rid of the plate glass windows we had on the bridge as they were very dangerous if hit. These windows would shatter and spray slivers of glass all around if hit by a bullet or a shell. They were great for vision but not very practical now that we were at war. There was also a rumor that we were going to have all our portholes along the hull covered which meant we could have lights on with out worrying about light leaks while out at sea. Life rafts were to be rigged on both sides of the bridge. They would be positioned so that when they were released they would fall into the sea with no obstructions. That is when we realized that if we were torpedoed our ship would sink very fast. We also heard that the anti-aircraft guns were going to be a Swiss model 20 mm rapid fire cannon. We wondered about our single shot 3 inch 23 caliber deck gun but found out that wasn't going to be replaced.

We left Honolulu Harbor and steamed straight over to Pearl Harbor. As we approached the channel I could see the main signal tower signaling us with their large blinker light. Since we had no qualified signalman I was chosen to answer all their inquiries. They blinkered the message, "Who are you and what were you doing here?" Right then we got off to a bad start communicating, they didn't recognize our ships designated number which was W152, a Coast Guard Cutter. I finally gave them our radio call sign NRMD and the name of our ship CGC Tiger. They finally figured out who we were and then told us they had a message for us and could they send it in semaphore (Flag Signals) form? I had enough practice in semaphore so I thought I could handle a short message. After they gave me the time and the date and all the headings I figured out that it was going to be a general message given to all ships that entered Pearl. The message was in five letter code groups. Why it was sent like this way I'll never understand but I guess that was the way of the Navy. It was a 200 group message and since I didn't have some one recording each letter for me I wondered should I stop them now and get some one to copy for me or should I let them go ahead knowing that I could get this message when we tied up at our berth. By not recording the letters I could let the signalman go as fast as he could, this was a way for me to let them think I was a whizz bang signalman and could copy any speed they sent. I noticed as he was sending the message he began to go faster and faster each time I signaled, "Roger go ahead with the rest of the message." At the end of the message I gave him a great big roger and thank you. I think the poor guy almost fell off the tower. We all laughed about this and thought this surely made us look good coming into a great big Naval Base on such a small ship!

When we got to our berthing place I found that we were tied up next to a two stacked destroyer, our berth was very close to the Ten Ten dock area. I went over to the destroyer's radio shack and asked the man on duty if they had that general message to all ships that were stationed in the harbor. The communication officer happened to be in the room and overheard my request. He came up to me and said "I can give you that message in plain language so you won't have to decipher it which will save you a lot of time and effort". We were surprised to find a Lt. nice enough to give us the message already broken down and thank him profusely. The message was all about regulations and dress while in the yard.

We closed down the radio operation and sent all our gear over to radio materiale at the base to be refurbished. We had many VIP Naval Officers board us to look over the ship. I guess they were trying to figure out what they could do to make her a little better fighting ship. The yard workers started working on her right away and we were warned not to look at any of the welding or cutting of metal with torches and such to protect our eyes. They began by cutting out the square windows on the bridge and sealing all the port holes on the main hull. This gave us time to wander around the yard to look at some of the damaged ships that had been hit during the Dec. 7th sneak attack. They were being righted and repaired as fast as possible. There were also ships just in that had gone through a sea battle in the South Pacific. One of them was an aircraft carrier which was badly damaged. Just as I was walking by, not to far from her, a sheet of flame went shooting into the sky and the whole side of the carrier seemed to be on fire. Apparently a welder working on the side of the hull sealing some breaks contacted a gasoline leak that caused this huge shooting flame. The welder had to jump off the scaffolding into the water to escape the flames. I don't know how he fared from this accident. This carrier also had a 5 inch 38 caliber anti-aircraft gun knocked out by a Japanese bomber that had been flying straight at their gun mount. This gun was mounted about midships on the port side and the Marine gun crew that was manning the gun had made a direct hit on it but the plane continued straight on in and struck the gun mount destroying it and killing the whole gun crew.

A little further down the line past the carrier a heavy cruiser that had been in the same task force had a huge hole in her bow section. This hole was so large that a freight train could have passed through it without touching the sides. Rumor had it that a twenty four inch torpedo had hit her. The force of the explosion was so great that it lifted the number two gun turret completely off its track and it was tilting at about a ten degree angle. While looking at the damage I noticed that all the officers were wearing side arms and looking very grim. This was rather unusual. They were working to open up the bow section ahead of the torpedo hole so as to remove the sailors that had been trapped in that section. The captain had sealed off that section, during the engagement, for the safety of the ship which meant that all those crew members in that section would not survive. The rest of the crew became very unhappy about this because they believed that those people in that section could have been rescued without the ship sinking. That was why the officers were wearing side arms, they were afraid that the crew might mutiny. This didn't happen thank goodness. I don't know what became of this incident and never heard any more about the end result. I guess it was really critical to keep the forward section sealed no matter what the crew thought of the action.

When we returned to our ship, we saw that there were many naval officers on board inspecting the work being done. The skipper was busily showing them all the changes being made, so we tried staying out of sight, since we weren't exactly dressed according to the yard dress code, they did see us when they were on the bridge looking down at us standing around on deck but they didn't seem to notice us, thank goodness. I should mention that we had found an open beer garden while roaming around the yard, so we weren't exactly sober when we came back to the ship.

Chapter 23.

Readying for Action.

All the work was done on the ship so we returned to Honolulu Harbor with the skipper telling me that we egressed (egress is a noun not a verb) out of Pearl, or something like that. I think he was giving me an English lesson.

We returned to the small shipyard and began cleaning and painting over all the welding and repairs that were made. After about a week in port we had everything cleaned up. The ship was restocked with all the necessary items, fresh water was taken on, and the fuel tanks were loaded.

While in port we all got Christmas letters and packages though some what late. I got a coffee can full of chocolate chip cookies that my mother had made. They were put up for grabs down in our sleeping quarters. Needless to say they lasted about five minutes and were gone! I never saw anything disappear so fast before. While in port we were discussing what to do about the decks being so slippery when wet? Someone suggested painting the steel decks and then sprinkling sand on them and paint them again to make a good rough surface to give us better traction. On our next patrol the skipper asked me, "Where could we get some good sand for the decks?" I told him that we could probably get the sand from the beach at Fort Derussy which was just around the corner from the harbor entrance. He then asked me if I wanted to take the whale boat into the beach to get the sand. It was with OK with me so I picked a rowing crew, mostly guys who had **a lot of rowing experience and** we started out for the beach at Fort Derussy. I chose the sweep oar rather than a rudder to steer the boat because I would have better control this way.

We were aware of the anti-boat barriers all along the beaches where the defense forces thought landings might be made. Most of the barrier was made of old rail road **tracks** that were curved and laid out so that a sharp spike was pointing seaward where a landing barge or what ever might approach. Then after that there was barbed wire to work through so we knew it was going to be a little hazardous. The breakers were fairly small and I was doing pretty well getting around the railroad spike when all of a sudden a larger wave caught us and we landed on a spike right in the middle of the boat. Being a clinker built boat (Over Lapped Siding design) she was pretty strong, we just hung up on the spike for a few seconds and the next wave picked us off the spike. We quickly rowed on into the beach riding a wave in like a surf board and landed on the beach. After inspecting the hull all I found was a little gouge in one of the planks on the starboard side which was where the spike caught us. What a relief to find out that there was so little damage. We scrambled out on the beach and shoveled sand into a couple of large buckets that we had brought with us. While we were filling up the buckets I noticed a soldier coming towards us out of no where. As he approached I said, "Hi" and he replied, "Hey, you can't take any of this sand!" This caught us by surprise, I answered, "Who says we can't"? His answer was, "my commanding officer says so". My reply was, "Please tell you commanding officer my exact answer to his order is, F...you be sure that you tell him in those exact words." He turned around and didn't say anything, so we watched him march off with my message. We loaded the rest of the sand we needed and shoved off the beach and rowed back to the ship with out any more trouble.

The next day we painted the deck and spread the sand out and completed the job by early afternoon. Of course the color we put on the deck was the traditional war time blue that the navy was using at the time. Even our white hats were in this color as we didn't want any bright colors to stand out while at sea. We never heard anything from Fort Derussy after the sand incident but I did tell the captain about the episode, we all had a good laugh over that one. I could never figure out why that CO didn't want us to take any sand. Maybe he was on an ego trip, who knows?

Chapter 24.

Gun Practice.

On this patrol we were going to test out our new 20 mm cannons. The arrangement was that the navy would send out a target plane pulling a red sleeve for us to try and hit. Every one was pretty excited that we were going to fire the new weapons. It was about 11 am and the weather was beautiful. We arrived at the designated area for this gunnery practice just off Barbers Point. Since I wasn't on a watch I decided to climb up on the flying bridge just above the wheel house, to watch the practice firing.

The sky was perfectly clear, it was a perfect day for anti-aircraft gunnery practice. The navy plane could been seen coming over our port beam at about an altitude of 500 feet, with a speed of about 100 knots. The plane looked like a typical trainer plane and the target sleeve was trailing about 1000 feet behind her. The first gunner to fire at the sleeve started to late and didn't lead the sleeve enough so he missed it by at least a good hundred feet. The noise from the gun was one of the sharpest blasts that I have ever experienced, my ears were ringing especially when the gun swung towards the bow as far as it could go. Thank goodness they had put stopper guides around the gun so that it couldn't be swung into the ship. Every one on the ship was giving firing advise to the poor guys trying to fire at the target sleeve. Most of us were yelling, "Lead the sleeve more, start it out with more lead." We could see the tracer shells which were every third shell so that you could see where your shots were going. The next gunner did the very same thing, he didn't lead the target far enough either. The blasts was very intense and once the gunner started firing he would try and follow the sleeve but never quite caught up with it. The noise was really an ear splitting sound to me being on top of the wheel house I was getting the full brunt of the noise from that cannon. One time I thought the gunner was going to sweep right past the limits allowed and shoot me right off the flying bridge so I quickly dove to the deck thinking he could really sweep past the iron guards that kept the gun from hitting any of the super structure. The next time the plane came around the gunner started firing and again he didn't even come close. Before he could complete his session the gun went into a hang fire mode. This meant that someone would have to remove the bad shell from the breech. My friend, Scott, by now a chief boatswain mate, had the honors of removing this lethal shell and tossing it overboard before it could accidentally explode in our faces! That was a scary moment for the whole gun crew. When that was done they then decided to try and exchange gun barrels just for the practice of doing it. Changing the barrels occurs when the gun is fired for a long session and gets very hot so it is prudent to change it for a cool barrel. The hot barrel is inserted into a large tube of water to cool off quickly. The crew member who removes the hot barrel has to wear big heavy duty asbestos gloves the barrels got so hot. This exchange system kept the gun in action during an attack. After about the fourth run the target plane returned to base. We had no need to ask for the results of our target shooting as we knew that we didn't even come close to the sleeve target. We all realized that we weren't very good at firing at planes and wondered what it would be like to have one coming at us at the speed of sound or some where's near that unheard of speed. We did see some of the new awsome Corsairs, the navy gull winged fighter plane and they nearly achieved the speed of sound when diving steep. They had just come into use around the end of 1942. The army didn't have any real fast fighters in the Hawaiian area but we heard that they had plenty of P-38 twin tailed fighters on the West Coast and in Europe. We weren't getting to much in the way of fighters in the Pacific as we saw it. We ended up going into Pier 4 feeling dejected because of the poor showing at gunnery practice. We were glad that none of our other Coast Guard ships were there to witness our poor showing.

Chapter 25.

White Sharks and Pineapples!

On our next patrol we got the Barbers Point to Diamond Head run. While slowly turning at the end of our run at the Diamond Head Buoy we noticed that a tug was coming up on us on the inside position. She was towing a large barge loaded with ripe pineapples that were stacked high. As she came abreast of us, the tender on the barge signaled with his hands that he would toss us a few pineapples if we wanted any. He started tossing us pineapples about the size of a soccer ball and they were a beautiful golden color. We all lined up along the railing catching as many as we could. By the time the barge went past us we had enough pineapple for the whole crew, I think there were about a dozen or so. Everyone had a large chunk of delicious fresh ripe pineapple. We enjoyed the feast immensely.

Our executive officer, Paddy O'Rouke, had spent some time over at the Naval PX while we were in port and had purchased a deep sea fishing outfit. He got the harness and a swivel for the end of the pole to rest in when he was trolling. The reel was a large Penn deep sea fishing reel and it was the type that you hooked up to a leather harness which you wore. He was very proud of this fishing gear and he let us know that no one was going to use it without his permission. However he told me I could use it any time he wasn't using it. So we set up a heavy plank between the dept charge racks on the stern and put the swivel holder in it so that the heel of the pole would take the pressure when reeling in a large fish. The outfit was supposed to be able to haul in at least a 750 pound Marlin. That was the record for weight on Marlins caught in the Hawaiian Islands at that time. I was thrilled to try a little trolling with this gear while we were on patrol between Barbers Point and Diamond Head. On our next patrol we did get the assignment between the two points so O'Rouke suggested that I should try my luck at trolling since I was off duty at the time. He decided that I should use a plug with feathers attached to it called an Hawaiian Wiggler. We were running about three knots, the best speed for ping patrol. I let out about two hundred yards of line when we got near the turn around point on our designated run when I felt a sudden jerk on the line, I yelled, "I think I've got a fish on!" By the feel of it, I didn't think it was a very big one. I started to reel it in very carefully, playing it so that I wouldn't lose it when we got word that we should proceed back towards Pearl Harbor immediately. So the skipper rang up for full speed ahead which was about 12 knots. All this time I'm trying to reel this fish in. I could see the fish bouncing around on the surface. I kept on reeling the poor fish in till I finally got it aboard the ship. You could see that the poor fish had drowned because of the force of the water going through its mouth and out of its gills, it never had a chance. The fish turned out to be a 25 lb Yellow Fin tuna, which would be considered a very small fish to catch with this sort of gear. There was enough fish for the cook to fry a half of a steak for every one in the crew. The meat was delicious and it sure was nice to have something fresh. The next day, full of enthusiasm I started to fish just as we were crossing the Pearl Harbor channel entrance. We had to slow down to let a large mine sweeper cross our bow. That was towing an acoustic line searching for acoustic mines, she was dragging this long line that was held up by an air filled tube and sent out a very strong sonic signal that would set off most acoustic mines. Soon after passing the long line I let out enough fishing line again for trolling. With the mine sweeper still in sight and out of harms way I felt a big hit on the line. The pole bent very hard and I knew I had a big one on this time I could hardly hold the pole and the line kept feeding out even though I had the brake set for a pretty hard pull. Some one on deck yelled to the bridge that I had a big one on could they slow down a bit because I was having a tough time hanging on to this one. When the ship slowed down the pressure on the pole dropped off rapidly and I shouted that I had lost him. Then the skipper resumed to the normal speed and again the pole bent almost in half. The pull was so drastic I thought I would lose the pole. The crew began gathering on the stern to try and get a good look at what was on the line. One seaman yelled, "It's a white shark!" When I heard that my heart started pounding because I started to believe I really had a big white shark on the line. I remember helping some one pull in a 12 foot shark off of Maui and this felt like the same kind of action. The skipper and the executive officer were getting kind of nervous as we had stopped almost in front of the Pearl Harbor entrance. They didn't think it would look so good for a patrol boat to be seen fishing while on sub patrol. I tried reeling in the fish as fast as I could but it was putting up lots of resistance and I couldn't figure out why I didn't feel any tugging or jerking at all. It was just as if it was submitting to its fate of be caught. I got the big fish reeled in about ten feet from the stern, with the crew hanging over my shoulder, giving me advice, like how to reel this big fish in and trying to identify what kind of a fish I had. It was quite exciting! Some one exclaimed loudy, "Hell its only a big ole white sack" sure enough it was a large sack about the size of a white flour sack and it was full of something. Boy! Did I feel like a big dummy. I thought I was going to be the big fisherman hero and it turns out that I looked like a big jerk. I reeled the sack in all the way and discovered that the sack contained about 50 rotten hot dogs, ugh! The whole crew gave me the hee haw and kept razzing me for the rest of the day which made me feel worse. Apparently the hot dogs had gone bad and the cook on the mine sweeper decided to chuck them over board as they cleared the channel. I guess he thought it would be OK to toss them in the drink rather than cart them around while on their mine sweeping mission. However we were warned never to toss anything overboard that might float because this would give a submarine a clue as to who was in the area and how large a ship it might be, I guess the guy who threw it over board figured we weren't out to sea far enough to give any clues to the enemy. After that day we all had a good laugh over the white shark episode and I continued to fish whenever I could. A few days later I hooked into another fish which had a funny shape, its lower part of its body in the mid section was pulled in as if it were sucking its stomach up. It looked like an albacore and was fairly large and had the bluish tint of an albacore. The skipper wouldn't eat any of this fish because he thought it was poisonous. We all laughed about that and was glad to eat his share of this one. I caught three fish on this patrol but never hooked into a marlin. I wondered what we would have done if I had connected with a big marlin that was too heavy to haul aboard. I guess we would have had to cut the line and let him go. After I left the ship for the states two of the crew members, Barnes and Burns, caught some very nice fish that looked like Mahi-Mahi.

With no refrigeration equipment on board it was nice to have some fresh fish to eat once in a while.

Chapter 26.

Midway

Around June 2, 1942, we started another patrol between Barbers Point and Diamond Head buoy. During this time we received a warning that a large Japanese task force was approaching the Aleutian Island and there could be another one heading for Pearl Harbor.

We were put on General Quarters which meant everybody had to man their battle stations. We were told that this would last while the threat was still possible. This meant that we had to stand by our stations until the alert was deemed as over. The captain even declared that we observe strict water rationing, meaning that there would be no fresh water showers or wasting of water except for eating and drinking. The second night out on this patrol some of the crew reported seeing one of the motor machinist washing his teeth in the scuttle butt located in the galley, a scuttle butt is a drinking fountain and was sort of where you got all of the rumors like hanging around an office water bottle dispenser. The whole crew let this machinist know that we didn't like him using water to brush his damn teeth. We embarrassed him so much that he quit that practice while on this particular patrol. After about seven days we were relieved of this patrol and we returned to our base at Pier Four in Honolulu. We then found out that there had been a fierce battle around Midway Island and that there had been tremendous losses on the Japanese side, especially in aircraft carriers and that we had heavy losses also. We lost the carrier Yorktown North East of Midway while the naval forces were trying to get her safely back to Pearl Harbor. She had a skeleton crew on board working hard to salvage her when a Japanese submarine sank her with a torpedo salvo. The Japanese lost four carriers and a lot of seasoned carrier pilots. It was basically a victory for us even though it all happened by a stroke of good luck on our part. I had lived in the little town of Novato, where Hamilton Air Force Base was located which was also where Major General Tinker had been the first commanding officer. I had gone to High School with Major General Tinker's son. General Tinker was now located in the Hawaiian frontier. I mention this because there was a rumor that he had lead a group of B26 bombers out to sea to search for that Japanese task force heading towards Midway Island and that they never returned. However I never had it confirmed and I have not heard anything about that mission since. I also heard that his son was killed in an Air Force plane crash down off of the Panama Canal about the same time as his father was lost. We returned to our home port in Honolulu at Pier Four, tired and happy that we were able to avoid any big confrontation with the enemy.

Chapter 27.

R & R.

After the ship was secured and things settled down to normal the skipper announced that the crew would be able to get R & R and that we would go in groups of four crew members at a time for seven days. I was lucky to be named in the first group. We were to go to the Royal Hawaiian Hotel for the seven days at a cost of 50 cents a day. The four of us that were chosen, quickly got ready to go. We packed a couple of changes of underwear and an extra pair of undress whites, the uniform of the day for liberties, and our toiletry gear, so off we went to the Royal Hawaiian Hotel. When we got to the hotel they told us all the rules and such things like when meals were served etc. They gave us the key to our room and we discovered that it was one of the bridal suites with a view of Diamond Head and the ocean off of Waikiki Beach. We saw that they had strung barbed wire along the beach and that there were anti-barge railroad spikes embedded in the sand about 100 feet out in the breakers. These spikes were placed at about every five feet so that they would surely catch a boat trying to come into this beach. It would have made it rather interesting if you wanted to try and use a surf board, which no one did. There was enough room to swim in the area before you ran into the spikes. After settling in we decided as a group we would leave the hotel and look for a liquor store and perhaps buy a bottle. When we got near a store the first thing that we encountered was a long line of people trying to get into the liquor store. We remembered the long line for cigarettes at the tobacco counter in down town Honolulu. we could only buy an off brand of cigarettes called Piedmont's that were originally meant for the Philippine Islands. But they were unloaded in Oahu because the ship couldn't go on to the Philippines. There was a great shortage of cigarettes, in fact all the name brands I was familiar with had disappeared inside of two weeks. Piedmont cigarettes were the only brand and they had to be stamped by the carton for their U.S. tax stamp before being sold because they didn't have the regular United States tobacco stamp on each package. We started groaning about the long line of liquor buyers and fell in behind a young couple who had arrived just ahead of us to stand in the line. We started a friendly conversation with them while shuffling along towards the door of the liquor store and found out that they were married and we got to joking and laughing around so much with them the husband asked us if we would like to go with them to his bosses house for a cocktail party. We thought that would be a great idea and told them so. After getting our own bottle of booze we climbed into their car and took off for the party. On the way over they told us that his boss was Chinese and was the CEO of a large hardware chain. We found out that he was part of the so called Big Five Group that ran the Islands. Most of that group was from the missionary families that came to the Island in the in the early days. He must have been an exception, since he was Chinese, maybe a favored converted Christian! When we arrived we could see that the house was very large and in a very fashionable neighborhood. At the door we got a big welcome from the host whom we could see was indeed of Chinese origin. After being introduced to the rest of the guest, we were offered food and drinks. Everyone wanted to hear about our war adventures, being well fortified with a couple of stiff drinks which we weren't used to, we started telling out and out lies about our adventures at sea! We rapidly became aware that the host thought that we were submariners because of our shields sewn on our right hand sleeves, the Coast Guard Insignia, so to make our story more interesting I made up a story of an experience that we had in Tokyo Bay! To make the story more plausible I used an account of some real submariners that I had read about in those reports that came in on submarine tactics in the South Pacific. They were thrilled to hear such stories and we kept a good part of the evening entertaining them with more and more colorful stories. When it was time to leave this fine party our newly acquired friends, our young married couple, invited us to finish out the night by partying at their house. Their house was located out towards Koko Head a few miles past Diamond Head in a very nice middle income neighborhood. When we arrived at their house I confessed to the fact that we were in the U.S.C.G. and the young wife just smiled and said, "Yes I know since I was married to a Coast Guard officer for awhile." After that we told her husband what we really did, antisubmarine patrol duty. We partied the rest of the night and had a great time, I don't think we ever got any sleep. After a nice breakfast and lots of coffee we started back to the Royal Hawaiian Hotel. We said our good byes and told them what a wonderful time we had and that we would see them again some time when we got back into port. Alas, we never saw or contacted them again much to our regret as they were great hosts.

Back at the hotel we found the beer garden for service men and had a good time exchanging real war stories with a lot of sailors from the Yorktown, the carrier that had been sunk during the battle of Midway. They were also staying at the Royal Hawaiian Hotel. They described how the ship fared during the battle of Midway. They had been hit very hard, in fact she was so bad off that they decided to leave her with just a skeleton crew to handle her since she could not accept any planes because of the damage on her flight deck. They described how she was sunk by a Japanese submarine while they were trying to get her fires out and rigged for towing. We couldn't top any of their stories and felt that we got away pretty easy during the battle of Midway. Another story the guys told us was about a Chaplain who had two life jackets on when there was a shortage of them. This made some of the crew very upset because here was an officer who wasn't helping the crew as he should have. How ever this could have been a false accusation because of mistaken identity of personnel under heavy fire.

In the afternoon we all decided to go swimming on the beach and posed for pictures on the beach and after that we took pictures of the view from our room. After dinner we decided to cruise around the bars that were close to the hotel. We had a drink in a bar on the beach side of Kapaloni Blvd and the waitress gave me my change, a dime, by dropping it in my drink, this made me mad so I didn't leave any kind of a tip. We left that joint and went out the black out door system into a very dark moonless night. Our eyes were adjusted to the lighting inside so we were walking along the sidewalk kind of blindly waiting for our eyes to get adjusted to the darkness when I walked into something very hard and sharp. My knee took the brunt of the blow, feeling down to see what I walked into I discovered that it was a fire hydrant right on the edge of the sidewalk, no wonder my knee felt so bad. I complained so much about the darkness that the gang decided we may as well go back to the hotel and get some rest. After that we spent most of our time swimming and playing on the beach. The day we left to go back to the ship we took many photos of ourselves in front of the Royal Hawaiian just to prove that we really did stay there. We returned to the ship and felt that we had a nice relaxed time for our R & R duty.

Chapter 28.

2nd Bombing.

As this tale is supposed to be told in the right sequence, this next episode happened in March of 1942, as I remember the action. Here we were out on another picket line patrol off of Pearl Harbor. The day was uneventful and became sort of boring. Several drills were held such as manning the anti-aircraft guns and getting to our stations on time. It was a dark and moonless night, the time was around ten pm when five or six search lights were turned on and they began to criss cross the sky. It was a very strange sight as we were in a total black out area. It looked like a Hollywood grand opening or the opening of a new super market. I was on the bridge on watch running the sonar gear. I hadn't picked up any thing that sounded like submarine activity. However there was plenty of dolphin noise's which sounded as if they were playing with the sonar ball under the ship. It seemed as if they were rubbing against the ball, there were plenty of squeals heard during this period.

We were wondering why the search lights were going when the thought came to us that maybe they detected an airplane raid coming into Pearl. If that is true we thought it was kind of dumb to have the search lights on as this did pin point where all the military targets were. When all of a sudden all of the search lights went out at the same time. In a few minutes we thought we could hear airplane an engine or propellor noise coming in from the west.

The skipper called me over and asked me to climb up on the flying bridge with a pair of binoculars and see if I could spot the plane. He offered the glasses to me and I grabbed them and dashed for the flying bridge which is just above the wheel house. I did leave the ping machine pointed straight ahead just to keep any sub nervous while I was on this lookout assignment. Starting up the vertical ladder along side the wheel house structure as fast as I could climb I made a quick hop off the ladder hoping to land in the middle of the deck. Unfortunately I forgot that a guy wire support for the signal mast stretched across that particular spot and I collided with the guy wire right across my nose removed a considerable amount of skin and brought tears to my eyes. I could feel a little blood running off my nose from the injury. As I got situated I threw the glasses up to my eyes and tried to spot the plane as I could hear the engines plainly now. Needless so say I was highly excited and my heart was thumping like a bass drum. I was shaking so bad I could hardly see through the glasses as they bounced around in my hands. The sky was so dark that I couldn't spot a thing. The skipper kept yelling from the wing of the bridge, "Do you see anything?" Just then a loud boom, boom, boom sounded. I didn't have to answer but the sounds came from a deeper location than down town Honolulu or Pearl Harbor, it was more like up in the mountain range behind Honolulu. The engines died out and sounded as if they had crossed over the ridge and flown on to their designated rendezvous. After that my heart beat slowed down to normal and I hoped that was the end of the bombing raid. This was as close to a purple heart award for me so far. I knew my nose was bleeding a lot so I quickly climbed back down to the bridge and applied a band aid to my nose from the first aid kit. When we got back to port after this patrol we read an account of the bombing raid. It seems that the plane dropped three 100 pound bombs or near that weight and missed the town or what ever he was trying to bomb. He did hit somebody's veranda or patio that hung out over a steep embankment, on the mountain side. Two of the bombs just hit the side of the mountain and the other one that hit the man's patio putting a hole through the deck but didn't go off until it hit the ground about a hundred feet or so down the embankment. This raid is barely mentioned in any of the naval books, that I have read. However, I did find a story by a Japanese Submarine Captain, that he had refueled two twin engine sea planes in preparation to bomb Pearl Harbor that time in March of 42. One of them had to return to base because of engine problems, which explains why I heard only one plane flying overhead that night.

Chapter 29.

Plane Crash.

It was a nice warm spring day and the sky was clear, we were on our regular ping patrol and working our way down to the Diamond Head buoy when we observed a A20A bomber just flying overhead giving off sounds like the engines didn't want to function. They had apparently just taken off from Hickham Field. They had just passed overhead when both engines quit. The pilot kept the plane in a straight line and started losing altitude. We all ran out onto the wing of the bridge to watch

236

it land in the water. The plane did a pancake landing, throwing a water spray over the fuselage with the tail tilting up and then settling down level in the water. We headed over as quickly as we could to rescue any survivors but another patrol boat was closer than we were so they had the honor of rescuing the air crew. We could see some one climbing out of the cockpit through the open hatch. It was apparent that they all had survived the crash. To our surprise the patrol craft started towing the A20A towards the beach. We heard later that the only one injured was the pilot. He had hit the instrument panel with his head and ended up with a broken nose and some cuts on his face. There were two other crew members but they came out unscathed. I don't know if they were able to salvage the plane as we all thought that it was a miracle that it could float so easily. I guess it had a very strong cover and that was why it didn't break up when it hit the water. Just a few days later a fighter plane flew over head with its engine on fire and was smoking badly. We all got very excited and wondered if he would make it to Hickham field. He evidently did and we couldn't help except if he had fallen in the drink before getting to the air base. We wondered why there was no communications system between all the military bases and ships. I guess we will never know. A couple of days later the crew asked the skipper if we could have a swim call out at sea as the weather was so nice we thought it would be fun. The skipper must have been feeling good because he said it was all right with him but we would have to have a shark lookout and the machine guns ready if one appeared. So the crew that wanted to swim dove in but stayed real close to the ship just in case. We could only stop for about 15 minutes and everyone that wanted to had a refreshing swim. On another day the crew asked for another chance to swim around noon time. This time one of the regular lookouts spotted a giant manta, the so called devil fish. This fish was huge and was feeding on a school of small fish like anchovies. The spread of its kite like structure was about 12 feet or better. Some one on the crew said I guess we won't go in swimming today and every one agreed. One of the machine gunners on the bridge got permission to fire the gun on it. He fired a burst of about 10 rounds and, of course, we knew that he couldn't hit the fish he would only scare it. That giant ray went from its horizontal feeding position to a distinct vertical position to dart away so quickly we were amazed at the speed it had attained.

On another clear day while slowly sweeping the area between Barbers Point and Diamond Head we could see the Saratoga, one of our biggest carriers at the time, coming in from the west and heading for the Pearl Harbor channel entrance.

After I made a complete sweep around the area I trained the listening part of the sonar on the Saratoga. She was about three miles from the entrance when I heard this loud explosion on the sonar speaker. To me it sounded like she had been hit by a torpedo. We tried pinging around her to see if we could detect a submarine lurking in the area but to no avail. The rumor was that she did get a torpedo hit on her way into the harbor but we really never found out if it was true or not. While doing this kind of patrol we had a chance to see many damaged ships come in to Pearl for repairs. Once in awhile we would see a submarine coming in off of a patrol with a broom tied to the periscope telling every one that they had a clean sweep of their patrol area in enemy waters. Other times we would see a new ship coming in or going out of Pearl Harbor. One day a new cruiser came out of the Harbor channel on what looked like a practice run. I didn't know if it was a heavy or a light cruiser but she had great looking lines, a formidable looking fighting ship. We were all impressed with the way she was pushing through the sea with a bone in her teeth,(that's the white foam off of her bow while traveling at high speed), making us believe that now we were getting some great new ships to help us in the Pacific war front. We were all remarking about how fast she was traveling as she went steaming past us on her way West over the horizon. With all of us doing our jobs on the bridge and watching her high speed performance, all of a sudden she made a 180 degree turn in an instant. It was something I'd never seen before, it was awesome. All I saw was a huge spot of white foam all around her stern and she was heading back to Pearl just like that, no problems at all, we were all amazed at this performance. I had never seen a ship come about that quickly before and wondered how any one aboard could keep on their feet or stay balanced when maneuvering like that.

We noticed that her gun turrets were laid out much better than the cruisers Atlanta and Juneau, a class of light cruisers that we said had a pagoda like silhouette and were very easily blown up when hit by a torpedo or a direct shell hit because of their ammo distribution setup. They had an ammunition elevator under each turret which meant that the whole ship was one big ammunition storage bin, as they had ten 5 inch 38 twin gun turrets on board. All that fire power was good but very dangerous. The Atlanta was blown completely up with very few survivors found. That was the ship that the five Sullivan brothers were on when they lost their lives.

Chapter 30.

Target Practice.

While cruising off of the north end of the island one day we were mistaken for a small target ship and became the target for a bunch of naval dive bombers. They were dropping small water bombs and smoke markers and we finally got them to stop before we got hit by one of their water bombs. In fact I recovered one of the water bombs and saved it for a long time hoping I could take it home with me if I ever got back to the states. I don' know how I would carry it back to the states because the darn thing was about 3 feet long and 12 inches in diameter and weighed about 15 pounds when empty it had a nice looking set of tail fins and looked like the real McCoy. Another time the navy was practicing torpedo runs with a few PBY flying boats and they mistakenly aimed their torpedoes at our ship. We were running about 3 or 4 knots doing a slow ping patrol when they started dropping ariel torpedoes aimed directly at us. I ran out on the wing of the bridge on the starboard side and watch one going directly for our midship position. Lucky for us they had set the depth a little lower than our draft or it probably would have stove a nice hole in our thin hull. The torpedo's had a yellow colored head on them which I guess made it easier to recover at sea. I believe after they have run completely out of fuel they surface for easy recovery. There were several PBY'S doing this torpedo practice run. We all wondered why they even thought that they could do an effective bombing run, as they were about the slowest plane to fly for the navy. I remember the difficulty the regular torpedo bombers had in trying to get in close enough to hit any thing before they were shot down during the battle of Midway. Anyway it made it an exciting day for us as our patrols were beginning to become very boring. About this time we saw our first Corsair fighters fly by us off of Barbers Point. What was amazing to us was the fact that we didn't hear their engine or propellor noise until they had run past our position. I was told that they feathered their propellers and cut their throttles when diving down towards our ship. They were a beautiful sight with their gull wing shape and big radial engines.

Since the midnight to 6 am shift was covered by enlisted men so that the officers could get their rest, we decided that we could break up the monotony by trading jobs during the night. Our highest rank was chief boatswain mate who happened to be my best friend Scott who wanted to run the sonar gear so we would trade, then our friend Jim Elliot the MM2C wanted to conn the ship so I volunteered to run the engine room while he took over the bridge. While down in the engine room I could hear Scott and Jim laughing and saying I wonder what Swede would do if we rang up slow astern on both engines. Just as I figured, they ran both port and starboard annunciators for slow astern! Jim had told me how to do this maneuver early on when I first came on board. So I shot the air to both diesel engines to shift the cam shafts for reversing the engines and started both engines in reverse much to their surprise. I felt pretty darn good being able to do this maneuver. Later on I heard the skipper asking Scott why we went into that engine change in the middle of the night? The standard answer was we thought we had a contact on the sonar and didn't want to lose it by running over it to early. He never gave us much of a quiz on something like that because if there was really a problem or contact we would have awakened him to take over. We did have fun trading jobs and we learned a little about the other guys job. We even had some time in the radio shack when there was nothing important going on the fox schedule. Radio phone messages or calls were about all that the others could copy, so if a CW signal came in like a fox schedule message a radio operator would have to quickly sit down and get it on paper with the typewriter. We would only do this kind of operation if it was a quiet evening, meaning there was no sign of a submarine or air attack on the Islands.

On this patrol we had orders to escort a small naval aviation gasoline tanker west towards the more vulnerable war front, the South Pacific area. We spent the first day just plowing away in a moderate sea when we ran into a large naval task force containing about 5 heavy cruisers including the Honolulu a square stern cruiser with a catapult launching device for scout planes. The first thing they did was fly a bunch of signal flags on the flag ships halyards which read, "designate course and speed", it took us about three minutes to figure out that message so we answered back to them the same way by raising the appropriate signal flags as to what our speed and course was. This made our skipper very nervous because he didn't want any thing to go awry in front of a big naval task force. They soon disappeared over the horizon leaving us alone with our tanker heading westward at about 12 knots. As darkness of the evening fell upon us the skipper issued orders to the effect that there would be no smoking on the bridge or any where top side. I guess he was worried about that task force in case we crossed their path. About 2200 (10 pm) we heard heavy gunfire and the launching of catapult planes. We all laughed when the remark was made that the SOC planes engines were 90% noise and 10 % power. We even had some shells flying overhead which made us very nervous. We assumed that it was just a practice session going on, since we didn't see any other ships around that looked like a Japanese force. We soon moved away from the scene and kept on going westward. We finally got to the point where we left our little gasoline tanker on its own and turned around to head back to Pearl Harbor. It must have been around midnight when we got an urgent Fox sked message addressed to us and info to the rest of the fleet. Since it was urgent I quickly set up the decoder to see what the message said. As I noted before, this type of cryptograph work was only handled by officers on all naval vessels except our ship. We never questioned the communication officer about this as I felt very important doing this type of work. Any how, try as I may the message came out garbled, so I told the skipper I might have set the machines pins up wrong and would have to reset them in order to break this message down. It still didn't come out right with the second try so I was getting desperate since this was an urgent message sent to us only. This is the highest priority message ever sent in the naval communication system, there is nothing higher. Everyone was getting upset. We had checked everything we could think of, I was beginning to think that we were using the wrong machine for this message when I noticed that the message was made up at 0000 (midnight), so I started experimenting with the dates and sure enough they had set up the message with the date of the day before, but used the new date for the key to set up the decoder. This time the message came out all right. The message sent was informing us to come into the Pearl Harbor area on certain grid lines so that the radar stations would know it was us and not some enemy warship. Since we didn't have radar or IFF equipment this was the only way they could recognize that it was our ship entering the area. This was only speculation on our part but it seemed like the right idea. However, we did arrive in the area around 0200 (2am). In the complete darkness you could hardly see the out line of the mountains behind Oahu. I hit the sack as we were nearing the Diamond Head Buoy and was trying to go to sleep real quick when I heard an awful racket going on topside. Jumping out of my bunk to find out what was going on I found everyone had hit the deck in the wheel house because that very same search light platform just south of the Diamond Head Light House had open fire with some heavy machine gun fire aimed directly at us. With tracers and bullets flying over the ship everyone had hit the deck to avoid getting hit and no one thought of reaching the recognition light switch which you had to crank manually so that the proper lights would blink on for identification that you were a friendly warship. Some brave soul finally got nerve enough to get up and crank the damn signal. The firing then ceased and we went back to normal operations with some one actually on the helm steering the ship. I went back to my sack and thought of the possibility of one of those shells coming through the hull where my bunk was located. However they must have been lousy shooters cause we never found a mark or any hits on the hull or super structure. We felt pretty lucky that we made it through that friendly fire but wondered how come that outfit wasn't informed about ships coming into their zone of operation. The next morning we proceeded into Honolulu Harbor and back to our Pier Four berth.

Chapter 31.

The Golden Rivet!

While in port it seems as if we get into all kinds of difficulties. This time one of our radio strikers, seaman Leon, was telling one of the new recruits who had just come aboard, all about the Golden Rivet and where it was located. No one was paying any attention to their conversation except to say, "Yes, there was a Golden Rivet located some where on the hull." This was like the Golden Spike they placed when they completed the rail road on the transcontinental rail line. I guess this mid

Western recruit believed Leon because the next thing I knew they were going to view the rivet that afternoon after noon day chow. Late that afternoon I heard this bloody scream and the new kid came running into the crews quarter wild eyed and breathing hard yelling something about killing Leon in the Lazaretto locker compartment. Boats ran immediately to the hatch and looked down into the darkness of the locker and there was Leon lying on the 5 inch hawser manila line with his face all bloodied up and struggling to get up. Several guys climbed down the rungs of the ladder to the floor of the locker and helped him get out of the compartment. Looking at his face, we saw that he had taken a pretty good whack on his left side. We asked him what had happened but he wouldn't talk about it, so we asked the new kid what he had hit Leon with? "I hit him with the flat of a fire axe that was hanging on the bulk head near the hatch because he was making unsavory advances on me and there was no Golden Rivet to be seen any place!" It dawned on us, that dumb Leon was just trying to scare the kid but he over did it and the end result was a smashed in face. Leon refused medical attention and laid in his bunk for about three days before he could get about the ship again. I guess he learned some thing from that little episode.

Then we had a real tragedy happen one early morning, while in port, when I heard a large bang from a forty five automatic pistol. This one was topside on the main deck right near the gang way. There laid Richard Heddy, a seaman 1st class, who had been doing the deck watch during the night lying on the deck bleeding from a bullet wound in the calf of his left leg. Because he had the deck watch, he carried a colt 45 for side arms. He used this gun for this sorry attempt to bring about a medical discharge. We found out that he was despondent over being out in the Pacific doing this war duty and being very homesick he thought if he could phony up an accidental wound so that he might be able to get transferred back to the states. When I got there I saw that the bullet had shattered his leg badly and that the bullet was imbedded in the wooden deck. Thinking that maybe he would want the bullet I dug it out of the deck and pocketed it for the time being. Later on the executive officer Paddy O'Rouke asked me for the bullet as they would need it for evidence when this mishap was investigated. I found out later that they consider this grounds for a bad conduct discharge and he would lose all benefits promised to all enlisted personnel after they got out. I felt sorry for Richard because not only was he losing everything, he was not going to recover the use of his leg because he had shot the main bone to smithereens, and it was made impossible to repair.

On another night I found that I couldn't sleep so I went on top side to look around when I noticed a small wake traveling inward in the middle of the harbor. I tried yelling General Quarters but couldn't seem to get any noise to come out of my mouth. Now I really was getting frustrated and began sweating profusely, when all of a sudden I hit my head on the bunk above me and realized that I was having a night mare! Again my old heart was beating like a trip hammer but I was happy to find out that it was only a dream. It sure seemed real!

Chapter 32.

The Navigator.

On the next patrol I found out that our skipper couldn't use the Polaris instrument because he couldn't see well enough to get the landmarks lined up in the sights. So he asked me to do it for him, which I did. He even had me shooting the stars with his sexton, which was a great thrill for me because I had taken a navigation course at the YMCA Hotel in downtown Honolulu while I had been doing duty on the Roger B. Taney. We got along very well now so he sort of treated me like a son. When the time came for efficiency ratings he wanted to give me a rating of 4.0 which is a hundred percent efficient but I objected to this because if I got transferred and they saw the impossible rating I held I would be subjected to all kinds of ridicule. He agreed to lower it to around 3.7 after a long discussion with me about the ramifications this would present when I left his command.

One day he came back from a long session at headquarters with the news that we were going to escort seven merchant ships out of the area well past the submarine danger zone. What surprised me was that he wanted me to plot the course and speed for these merchant mariners. I was told that the speed was set for 12 & half knots and where we were to escort them. So l went to the chart desk and began laying out the course figuring wind and current speeds and drifts so that we would end up in the proper area after a two day escort. The course was set for a run West just a little off of Midway Island. This was very exciting for me and I laid out the courses we were to take and plotted the whole thing, then showed it to the skipper. He looked at it and said, "It looks fine to me, lets go with this plot, Swede." The next morning was the time to assemble the convoy. We moved out beyond the channel and began to get the freighters lined up. The skipper had me blinker to the ships, "Prepare to run at 12 & half knots on this course." A British collier, a wood and coal burning ship who was belching much black smoke began to blinker back to me that he wanted to talk. I responded with a "K" which means "Go ahead and tell me what you want." He came back with this, "You are an optimist, our best speed is 7 & a half knots." This made the skipper very mad because he said at the conference with these same skippers it was his understanding that all the ships could travel at 12 &

a half knots. This was going to make the convoy run very slowly indeed it did because we could still see the island at dusk that evening. I felt a little bit funny knowing that it was I who had plotted the course for this convoy, not some highly qualified navigator. I thought wouldn't some of those old grizzled freighter captains be a wee bit ticked off if they knew a second class petty officer with a rating of radioman had laid out the course we were on. At the time I was running the sonar gear and things were going along smoothly. We all changed shifts around midnight and I was headed for the sack when a Very pistol flare lit up the sky ahead of us. Things were happening on the bridge and the skipper called me back to work the night blinker gun, so we could inquire as to what caused one of the ships to send up that emergency flare. As we sped up to the lead ship I began working the ship that sent the flare up. We all converged on the starboard side of the bridge out on the wing to work the blinkers with the ship that had sent the flare. There wasn't much room and I stepped right on the executives sore toe, he let out a yelp and I tried to get off his toe and work the signal gun without losing to much time. He got over the hurt but was still cursing me for stepping on his foot.

The ship in question said that the look out had sighted a submarine on the surface about 7 o'clock off of his stern. I reported this to everyone and we all realized that this is where our ship was when the flare shot up into the sky. We acknowledged the message from the merchant ship and said we would investigate. However, knowing what we knew we decided that the lookout who had thought he had spotted a submarine probably had come out of a well lighted interior area. He probably had that night blindness that you get when you come out of a brightly lit room to a dark area like the darkness on the high seas on a moonless night. The next morning we dropped off the convoy and returned to Honolulu.

Chapter 33.

Star Shells.

While in port the skipper asked me to drive him out to the naval ammunition storage dump. The ammunition dump was located on the north west end of the island way past Barbers Point, of course I agreed to do it. How could I refuse? It was something different to do while in port. You see, I had an Hawaiian auto drivers license and this was a good time to use it. The skipper said that we had to get some star shells for our 3" 23 cannon. I guess the navy told him to go get some before our next patrol. So off we went in our old dilapidated pick up truck from the light house repair service shed on Pier Four. After driving through Ewa we came to one of those big circles that the British designed for cross roads and the skipper told me to go left which I did. About then I realized we were going the wrong way but since there was no traffic at all I kept going around until we got to the right roadway going out to the ammunition dump. However, there was a red light coming up behind us now and I was told to pull over. Looking at the vehicle I saw that it was a military police car. Out came an Army M.P., who begins to give me the riot act, as if I were some kind of fiend. So all I could do was ask him what the problem was. He replied, "You were going the wrong way around that turn around intersection and I have to give you a ticket." I looked at the skipper and he answered for me telling the M.P. that he instructed me to go that way. The M.P. looked kind of dejected and said, "OK, sir, I guess we can forget about it but remember you have to stay on the right when going around these circles. I sure was relieved that the skipper spoke up on my behalf, I had visions of a big fine for violating some military law. We continued on our journey to the naval ammunition storage dump. We picked up the star shells and the return trip was uneventful. All the time I was on the Tiger, we never fired our 3 inch 23 caliber cannon. We never fired a star shell, that I could recall, after obtaining those few we picked up that day. The skipper never explained why we suddenly needed those star shells. And I never asked! I imagined that they could be used as some sort of warning signal or maybe to create enough light to see an object on the surface of the ocean?

Chapter 34.

Cannon Boom, Boom.

On one of our patrols we happen to be in a good position to watch the navy test out some cannons that were taken off the Oklahoma, one of the Pearl Harbor raid victims. I believe that they towed her out to sea and sank her after taking all worth while equipment off. The cannons were 14 inch caliber, I think, and the brass decided to install them on shore as a good battery to protect the entrance to Pearl Harbor. It was around 10 pm when they started firing the guns. To our surprise

267

we could see the shells sailing through the air on their way out to sea. They had an orange glow like the glow of hot iron that comes off the blacksmiths charcoal fire. After the boom of the cannons the next sound was the shells flying through the air, it was an awesome sound, they sounded some what like a huge freight train that was passing over a trestle with us standing underneath the trestle. That's as close as I could get to the description of that sound. We all shuddered at the power and destruction force of those shells. They fired several rounds then quit for the night. They must have considered it a good job because they didn't do it again during the time I was stationed in that area.

Chapter 35.

Short Stories!.

We were taken from patrol to work with a naval transport which was involved in training marines in the art of landing on a beach head. We picked up the transport outside of the Pearl Harbor entrance and started to screen for submarines as she headed north towards the Makaha Beach area. We covered them the whole day while the marine's practiced landing on the beach through some pretty heavy surf using Higgins type landing craft. About 4 pm they signaled that it was time to go back home to Pearl. We started out going about 13 knots when the transport decided that this wasn't fast enough, they upped the speed to around fifteen knots so we started to fall behind them which is not very good for screening submarines. The skipper rang down to the engine room to up the rpm's on both engines. Then the engine room responded by yelling through the voice tube from the engine room that we were at maximum revolutions now. The skipper demanded that we force the engines higher which the engineers reluctantly did but first telling the skipper that it was not a good thing to run the engines above their red line. The skipper was red faced and mad and told the engine to go ahead and run them as hard as they could be driven. In the meantime we the crew were standing around on deck watching the navy transport outrun our ship. We could hear the engines straining all their worth. The exhaust pipes for the engines came out of the stack in the middle of the ship. Pretty soon the paint started peeling off the smoke stack because of the heat from the over driven engines. Finally we got back to the Pearl Harbor entrance and we slowed down and limped back to Pier Four our home base. The next day we went into the small dry dock near our base and started to repair both engines as both of them had burnt out main bearings. The black gang had to tear them down to get at the bearing's on the motor's and it took about a week to overhaul both of those engines. My friend Jimmy, never forgot that episode being a machinist mate and always interested in keeping engines running smoothly. We the crew appreciated the time out and enjoyed some extra liberty during this repair period. I was amazed at how they could repair those engine as quickly as they did. The skipper never got a reprimand for his demands on those engines!

One story that I heard while in port or read about was the one about our depth charge detonators which had depth setting starting at 100 feet up to 300 feet or more, we heard that they had started issuing a new model that could go off at a depth of 75 feet. Along the coast off Makaha beach to Barbers Point the depth of the waters was less than 100 feet and several destroyers had dropped depth charges along this area when making contact, by sonar, of what could have been a submarine. Since the depth was less than 100 feet these charges never went off so they lay there inactive but dangerous. I don't know how many of these depth charges were lying around that area but one of the new destroyers made a contact in the same area and happen to have the new detonators that could be set at the 75 foot depth which she set for this run. When the first charge went off the whole ocean seemed to explode as it set off all those other depth charges. It must have almost blown that destroyer out of the water. However there was no submarine debris so what ever those destroyers were picking up in that area must have been either a hot water jet or a coral head or even a cold water stream coming up to the surface., I never had the story really confirmed but it sure sounded plausible. Do you remember, I referred to a ship called the Azurlight, a converted yacht about 130 feet long at the water line. She was converted into a offshore patrol boat with similar patrol duties to our ship. On our patrols we would cruise past each other all day and all night between Barbers Point and Diamond Head buoy. We could hear each others sonar pings as we passed each other. This ship would challenge us every night as we passed her which got to be a pain because she would challenge us and we would have to give the pass word signal for the night by hand blinker. Each time I would have to stop and grab the gun and send the signal. After about three nights of this we, on the midnight shift, we decided not to answer anymore. It seemed to work because they didn't do anything about it when we didn't respond. The next time in port when the ole man went out to Pearl for a conference he caught hell for not responding to the Azurlight's challenge. So he came back storming at us about not giving the proper answer to the Azurlights challenge, saying we would have to answer every time. We complied but I said that this sure would give an enemy submarine a chance to pick up the challenge code for the night and couldn't those dummies recognize our ping signal as we passed by because we knew when ever she was in our area. On that same patrol we ran into some very strange ships coming around the Molokai Channel. I picked up their ping signal, from their escort, so I went manual on our ping machine and keyed it like a radio transmitter and asked the escort ship if he could read CW, the answer was that he could, so I asked him where had they come from and his answer was from the Great Lakes and these Great Lakes ferry boats were being used as transports. We could see that the bow of the ships were built like ferry boats and they had boarded up the openings and sandbagged the bow so that no water could get through to the lower deck. I thought we must be badly off if we had use these things out here in the South Pacific.

On our next patrol we were sent out with the Reliance and three Great Lakes Built patrol boats. . They were larger than we and had more armor than we did and more speed. I believe they were 185 feet in length and had a speed of about 16 knots. They were diesel powered. These ships were built on the Great Lakes and were built in a novel way. They started building them upside down and then turned over to complete the job. After they were ready to go to sea they were sailed down the Mississippi river down to New Orleans and out to sea. We were sent out to sea to practice sweeping for submarines. While out there we ran into some very heavy weather. We were running in waves that were about 20 feet high which made footing very hazardous on deck, people were slipping and sliding around, it got pretty damn miserable that day. At one point I looked over at our sister ship, the Reliance, and exclaimed, "I'm glad I'm not on her, look at how much she's rolling and pitching!" All this time I was hanging on to the bridge railing trying to maintain some semblance of balance. Everyone on the bridge started laughing at my ridiculous remark. The next morning the sea was calm, in fact it was as smooth as glass. Looking over at the Great Lakes ships I was surprised to see that their hulls were stove in between each rib, looking like a bunch of starved horses. The good old Reliance showed no signs of being in any kind of rough weather. This made us feel pretty good as it told us that we could weather any storm much better than those new ships they were building. Digressing a bit, I have to tell about our story telling and such while in port. During the evening when we weren't on liberty or going to the movies we would sit around a discuss every thing from movies to the war. One night I remember vividly was when Scott and I were discussing football and we started naming players who were All American from Stanford, California, Notre Dame and U.S.C. As we were naming these players a motor machinist mate by the name of Marshall butted into our conversation saying he remembered all those guys we were talking about. So Scott, being the devilish type, started naming phoney players and Marshall kept on saying, "Yeah, I remember him," I started the same thing by giving out names like Baergary, Gambolini, Zaterney, and said, "Yeah remember the great Zonkawiz that half back from Pittsburgh University, This brought much muffled laughter from the rest of the crew that was listening to this conversation.

On a serious note one night we started telling of our experiences during the surprise attack on Pearl Harbor. First Orvile Delaney told his experience starting with the fact that he had just gotten out of boot camp and was transported over to Pearl Harbor on the Cruiser Honolulu the square stern type that carried a scout plane on the fan tail. The plane was launched off of a catapult, then picked up right off the stern, the main reason for its being squared off stern. He told of the fast trip they made; it took them only four days to make it to Pearl from San Francisco, which is going pretty fast. They arrived in Pearl on the 6th and he was transferred to a barracks to be transferred to the Coast Guard the next day Sunday the 7th of

December. He told us of getting up, getting dressed to go to the mess hall for breakfast. It was about 8 am when he started walking over to where the mess hall was when he noticed gravel kicking up all around him. At first he didn't know why, then he saw the planes firing at everything and he realized that something was wrong. And he hit the ground. Lucky for him he didn't get hit. After it was all over he was sent to the Tiger as one confused boot. Can you imagine coming out of boot camp, riding on a high speed cruiser then being greeted with a hail of bullets after you arrive! Anyone would be confused I think. Then I told my part about seeing the three Japanese Planes and thinking they were Army and so on. Then Scott told about how they were on Patrol in front of Pearl Harbor just about parallel to Hickham Field when a low winged two place Japanese plane flew past them with the observer shooting at them with a machine gun and not hitting them. He said, "I could have hit those guys with a potato they were so close and flying so low". Robert Burns told us that he was working in the yard at Pearl Harbor and he decided right then he had better join the navy and help deal with those guys. He then told us he tried joining the Navy but they were too busy or something so he went next door and the Coast Guard took him in immediately. I remember when he came aboard the Tiger in his civies he sure looked out of place. We wondered why he wasn't in uniform at the time. The Coast Guard didn't have any small stores ashore for recruits so he had to come aboard in his civilian clothes. We all felt sorry for him and started giving him clothes so that he would look like the rest of us till he could get his own uniforms from a ship carrying such gear, like the Robert B. Taney. Poor Robert had been on board about two months when he collided with the combing on the stair well going down into our crew quarters. About 3 or four days later he had a mysterious attack of paralysis on his right side of his face. We all thought it was from his bump on the head but it was never confirmed. He did see Naval doctors about this malady but they didn't do much for his condition so he worked on the ship with this frozen right side of his face which made him slur his words, it eventually went away but you could see where the paralysis had been for the rest of the time I was on board the Tiger. We eventually found out that it was cause by an infection of the inner ear and was called Bell's Palsy. He told me that he had a second attack of it in the 1980's but this time they recognized the symptoms and cured it fairly quickly. He said that if they had known what it was the first time he would have had a complete recovery with no sign of the paralysis. We even got into a discussion of what we would do if we captured a Japanese submarine or what we would do if we were captured by them. We talked a good fight but I wonder what we would have really done if we got caught in a scenario like that.

While we were in port the petty officers stood most of the officer of the deck watches. This meant we had to carry side arms which was a 45 Colt automatic pistol. Each time we change shifts we had to unload the pistol by taking out the cartridge holder and pull the trigger of the gun while pointing it in the air to prove there was no bullet in the chamber. Well, one night I had the duty and was relieved at about 10 pm. We got to talking about various things, so in my usual manner I pointed the pistol into the air and pulled the trigger, lo and behold the damn gun went bang! I thought oh I forgot to dump the cartridge out of the handle, so without any loss of motion I fingered the cartridge release and caught the case in my left hand and my relief missed the whole action. Everyone on board came running out to the dock to see what had happened. We said that a bullet must have stuck in the chamber and went off when I pulled the trigger, that's the way its supposed to work, right? My relief said, "Yeah and the cartridge was ejected cause I saw it in Swede's hand". Lucky for me it was dark and he missed me dropping it into my left hand. Boy, that was some dumb mistake that I never made again. I was also lucky that I caught the case when I ejected it cause if I hadn't my relief would have heard it hit the ground, then I would have been exposed as to my stupidity.

Early in 1943 we got a few new recruits on board straight out of boot camp. Being a good fellow I thought it would be a good time to start chewing some shredded pipe tobacco as we put out to sea for our next patrol. I've never seen boots turn green so fast as we entered the open sea. In the mean time I felt that I had gone far enough with the chewing so I went out to the port wing of the bridge and hocked away the wad of tobacco, not realizing that the captain was coming up that side of the ship to the bridge, the wind picked up my wad of tobacco like a feather and dropped it right on the skipper's white hat with all the gold braid on it. Seeing what had happened to my wad I ducked into the bridge and quickly pretended to be interested in pinging the sonar as if looking for a submarine out in front of the ship. The skipper came into the bridge complaining about those gad darn seagulls, saying they ruined a good hat. I agreed, saying that we had that same trouble when we took the ferry from Sausalito to San Francisco. Was I glad that he didn't know it was my wad of tobacco that did the damage.

Chapter 36.

Swim Contest!

While in port refueling and picking up stores like fresh milk, fresh fruit like apples and oranges, etc, we spent a good deal of time sitting around on deck talking about things we could do, so we all started bragging about how well we could swim. Those that came from Hawaii thought that they could swim the fastest and the best. Burns claimed that he was Maui's best high school swimming champ and several guys from Oahu that were stationed on the Kukui claimed that no main land sailor could beat them, so we got into a big argument over this and the only way to settle it was to have a swimming race. Scott knew that I could swim pretty fast cause we use to swim over to Sand Island and back to Pier Four just for fun and I could beat him easily. So we decided we would have a big race by swimming across the water to the next pier where a big transport was tied up, which was about 75 yards away and then back to the Kukui, our starting point. Well things got hot and there was a lot of betting going on and most of the money was going on the Hawaiian swimmers, the exception was Scott who laid a bet on me, not very much, but just enough to make it interesting. Everyone one on the pier was watching when we lined up on the work deck of the Kukui to start the race. I figured that I would have one heck of a time keeping up with these guys because most of them had been swimming all their life in these waters. So, when they called the, on your marks, get set, ready, GO! I dove off the ship in a very flat dive almost like a belly flop and started swimming as hard as I could go using the American Crawl style which I had perfected a long time before I got into the Coast Guard. I tagged the big transports side and turned around to come, took a quick look to see how far behind I was, when I saw that every one was still coming towards me I knew that I was ahead by at least 10 yards so I just did a nice easy crawl and won by such a large margin, so that we never heard another word about how wonderful and great the local swimmers were.

Another in port session I wanted to go ashore but really didn't have the right to go on liberty but since we didn't have to run sonar or stand radio watches in port I thought maybe I could convince the executive officer Paddy O'Rouke that I needed church liberty. So I entered the ward room and asked to see Mr. O'Rouke. He asked me what I wanted, so I requested permission to go ashore on church liberty. He looked at me kind of funny and, "Said are you really going to go on church liberty?" I could see his face was getting kind of red and thought to my self Oh, Oh, I don't think this is going to play. So I said, "Hell no but I thought it would be an easy way to get off the ship," he started laughing and said, "You SOB if you would have said yes, that you were going to go on church liberty, I'd have kept you on board for the rest of our port side stay but since you were honest enough to say what you really wanted I'm going to let you go on that liberty." So off I went to the nearest beer garden, which was near the Aloha Tower.

Just before I got to the beer garden I heard a loud shot coming from that area. On arrival I saw an army Sargent sitting down in a tent looking very dejected. Wondering why, I soon found out that he had been cleaning his 45 automatic pistol and accidently fired it. Unfortunately he had it pointed at a low level and the bullet hit a sailor who was having a glass of beer at a table just out side of his tent, the bullet hit him in the head killing him instantly. That ended the beer drinking for the day. So, I went back to the ship thinking that I could have been hit! I later found out that the victim was a Coast Guard man. When ever we went on liberty we had to wear or carry a navy gas mask, which was regarded as an unnecessary burden by most of us. We soon learned to take the gas mask out of the pouch and just carry the pouch empty. One night I had the bright idea to fill the pouch with beer just before coming back to the ship. Knowing full well that was not a very good idea but it would be fun to see if I could carry this mission off. The pouch was lined with a rubber coating so it could safely hold any liquid. I did get it aboard ship with no trouble at all but nobody was anxious to try the beer so I dump it out over the side. The main problem with carrying the stuff was the fact that I had to walk very cautiously other wise the beer would spill out with every step.

On another occasion, while in Pearl Harbor for an over night stay, the crew got the bright idea to hang all our blues out for airing. These clothes were never worn in the tropics, so everyone who went past our ship thought we were ready to go back to the states. When asked we would say, "Yes why do you think our blues are getting aired out for?" It didn't take much for us to try a little something to start a big rumor, it even had us believing that maybe we would be going back. While in Pearl Harbor we used to watch movies that the large cruisers and battleships would run. We would stand on the dock side and watch the movies if it were a good one. You could hear the audio very easily, the one movie I remember was titled "Tobacco Road" and I thought it was a great movie. The part that drove me crazy was when the nephew just ruined a brand new model A ford coupe by smashing it to pieces with a sledge hammer. Another scene that I'll never forget was when the uncle or neighbor tried luring the young lady into his house with a bunch of turnips as the prize. I think I saw this movie once before in the states before I joined the Coast Guard. We all enjoyed movies no matter if the picture was an old one or not. We always got an intermission since they used only one projector and had to stop down and thread a new reel on to continue the story.

Chapter 37.

Sonar Drill!

In the early part of the year "1943", the navy decided that we should participate in the submarine simulation project where we would stage encounters with submarines while running sonar equipment on destroyers. They had us working with submarine crews so that the simulations was as close to the real thing as you can get. I remember working one crew from the Argonnaught that was pretty good they were the crew off of the Argonaught. Just after that I think they were lost on the next patrol trying to rescue a bunch of nurses from a tiny south Pacific Island. We did fairly well with the Ensign from the ship conning the destroyer and with me running the sonar and a seaman doing the helm or wheel duty. The next time out our captain, Lt. Jackson, said he would like to try doing the conning. He was a bit worried about how to go about it and on the way out to the submarine base at Pearl Harbor, he kept asking me. To put him at ease I said that if he did any thing that seemed way out I would quietly let him know the correct procedure and go on from there. He said, "O.K. since you are familiar with this simulation work correct me if I'm tracking the submarine wrong." We were driving over to the submarine base in our old Coast Guard pick up truck during this discussion, just the seaman, myself and the Captain. My answer was, "I'll do the best I can Captain," knowing full well I couldn't make him look bad in front of the whole group at the sub base.

We arrived at the simulation room and were told that we would be using a two stack type destroyer for this exercise. This meant that we would be driving a destroyer that could run at about thirty two knots and had side mounted depth charges besides the stern rack depth charges. This meant that we would have to visualize what it was like to run a destroyer. I figured that we would have a tough time doing this but if we didn't get too rambunctious we could get through the exercise O.K. In the simulation drill the course of the destroyers and the submarine are marked and traced on a long piece of paper so that you could see exactly how you went about your attack. It Showed every depth charge pattern that was laid out and so forth. We started out the drill by searching for the sub at a speed of about 12 knots and picked up the sub about 2000 yards off of our starboard bow. Being the sonar operator I yelled "Contact" and gave the gyroscope bearing position of the submarine. The skipper immediately told the helms man 30 degrees right rudder, I counter manned this command by saying in a whisper, no Sir, try 10 degrees right rudder don't turn so hard. We may lose him if you do. Come up on him gradually." The skipper did as I suggested and when we got in a good position to drop depth charge I said drop, "Two stern charges now, which he did. Then about 10 yards further I said, "Discharge both side charges which he did. Then about ten yards further I said drop two more stern charges." We ran eleven more attacks that day using that same attack and then waited for the results of our simulated attacks, which were traced out on a long piece of paper showing every run and how we did. A Lt. came out with the paper diagrams and told the skipper that was the highest score ever run at this facility so far. It meant a gold star for our skipper. We left to go home with the rolled up score on paper which he proudly carried back to our old pick up truck and we all climbed in not saying anything but could see he was very proud of what we accomplished. As we were driving down the road towards Pier Four, with me driving, the skipper spoke first by saying that was a great session and I want to thank you Swede, in fact I would like to give you something for that effort what would you like, I'll give you anything you want within reason. I thought for a minute and said, "I would like to go back to the states." He said, "do you mean a leave, which I can give you?" "No, I would like a transfer back to the states." He asked, wouldn't I like to just take a 30 day leave at home not counting travel time to get there then come back to ship after that. I replied "no, I would rather just get transferred back to the states and take my; chances." We returned to the ship and I didn't get an answer from the skipper, so I figured that was the end of that request I thought maybe I should have asked for some other kind of favor.

Chapter 38.

In Port At Pier 4.

When ever we were in port we had lots of clean up work to do. Like scrubbing down the decks and keeping all the lines and gear shipshape. We all had laundry to do since the cook quit taking our laundry or rather we quit giving him the job after the scorpion episode. We would drag our clothes out onto the dock in a bucket and fill the bucket with cold water and a bar of yellow soap and squish the clothes around with a sort of metal plunger on a handle like a plumber's helper. This metal plunger had holes punched in it to allow the water to squish through when we pushed down the clothes in the bucket. If you worked hard enough it got the clothes pretty clean. Our dungarees never really got too dirty but it took out all sour smells and such. Also, anything we wore at sea had to be colored, so all our white hats were dipped in blue paint, the same coloring we used on the ships hull. Everyone strived to look salty so the guy who had the most frizzed up looking hat was deemed to be the saltiest guy on board. On our ship, while working you could wear your hat any way you liked. The brim could be folded down in front like robin hood's hat or the brim could be pulled down all the around. Or the regulation way, brim up and tilted forward on your head, or back to give you that careless looking pose. Another thing that we had going while in port was card games. Since we didn't have such things as movies or even a radio, those of us who didn't go ashore for the night, would sit in the mess deck and play cards for what we called, "pay day stakes". All I can remember about those games was the night I was dealt a Royal Flush and another player had four of a kind! That was the night I got even for a lot of losses.

Once in awhile we would play Black Jack but we soon realized that the big winners were the guys who dealt the cards. Of course, you could take the deal when you had a Black Jack if you chose.

When both the Reliance and our ship were in port and tied up at Pier Four we would gather around on the dock and exchange sea stories. One night the O.D., from the Reliance, a coxswain, came over and started complaining about how lousy the skipper of his ship was. It was then that we discovered that he was as drunk as could be, which unnerved us as he had his forty five automatic out of his holster and was showing everyone one how he was going to shoot the old man. I happened to be on duty as the O.D. on our ship that night and the jerk came over and pointed that damned gun at me and said, "that is where I'm going to shoot him." I nervously pushed his hand out away from me and said don't point that gun at any one around here. Get the hell back on board your ship before you get into deep trouble and forget about the old man, your're drunk you dumb idiot." We got some of his crew to strip the gun from him and put him in his sack. Thank goodness nothing came of that nights action. As enlisted men we kept quiet about things like that. That guy never did gain any respect from either crew after that episode.

One morning an Army Sergeant came over to our ship in answer to an advertisement Scott and I had run about selling our little sail boat, a genuine Class Snipe. It was made out of Philippine Mahogany planking and was a great little sail boat.

As much as we hated to part with it we couldn't take care of it and we couldn't leave it anchored off in the harbor behind Pier Four where there was a little beach, as a lot of little Hawaiian kids swam out of there and they used our boat for a diving platform. So we sold the craft to that Sergeant and asked him where he was going to keep it and so forth. He said, "I'm going to put a bow sprit on her for more sails and maybe sail her to the States some time." We told him he was going to ruin a class boat and he would never make it back to the states in a boat like that. I don't know if he ever tried it but we never heard of anyone trying it, although some one had sailed a 16 foot craft from Treasure Island in San Francisco to Maui at the end of the San Francisco World's Fair some time around early 1940 and made it.

Chapter 39.

A Welcome Change!.

On one escort trip we were taking a tanker south past Hawaii the last Island in the chain going south. Mauna Loa always looked majestic with its snow capped peak and you could see the whole mountain from the top clear down to the waters edge. On this particular day with nothing to do but sun my self on deck, I noticed one seaman hanging over the bow and looking down at the water. Going up to him I asked him what he was looking for. He said the water is so clear I can see porpoises swimming just below the surface just ahead of us and once in awhile one of them will lay it's tail against the stem of the bow and let the ship push him for a few hundred yards. So I went up and hung over the side to look and sure enough there was a porpoise lying on his back and letting the ship push him along. This was an amazing feat as far as I was concerned, I wondered if it really was happening, as they could have been just swimming along at the speed of the ship making it appear that they were being pushed, because when they got tired of that position they would dart out ahead of the ship with a fantastic burst of speed that was almost unbelievable. That really made an impression with me since I was familiar with their actions around my sonar ball under the ship. About that time a lookout reported that a twin engine seaplane was coming up on our stern. Looking back over the stern I could see this low flying seaplane making an approach as if he were going to strafe the ship. Some one exclaimed, "It looks like a Jap flying Betty"(a two engine flying boat) So we went into General alarm and watched as it approached the ship. When it got much closer we could see that it was one of our PBY'S. We all thought what a dumb way to come up on the ship, we could have fired at it and knocked it down, lucky for them we held our fire. They waved at us as they passed by! This had to be a very uneventful patrol. So back to Pier Four we went and tied up for a rest and supplies.

What an exciting day this was for me, the Captain told me I was getting a transfer back to San Francisco in about two weeks. This was in the spring of a 1943, April. So the first thing I thought of was, "What am I going to do with all those Postal Saving certificates I had save'd all during my time in the Islands?" So 1 went into my locker and gathered up all of the certificates and headed for the main post office down town in Honolulu. There were only a couple of windows open and I found out when I finally got to the window that I would have to sign every certificate I wanted to cash in which was all of them. They were mostly ten dollar ones with a few for one hundred dollars. Those were the ones I bought when I shipped over in 1942, that was one hundred dollars for every year I had to ship over for, which was three years, so I had three hundred dollars. I could hear lots of grumbling over the amount of time I was spending at the window. The postmaster was helping me and it did take quite awhile to sign all of them and add up the interest and the total amount. It came to a little over fifteen hundred dollars. Now I was in a dilemma, Martial law said that no one could carry more than two hundred dollars in cash on their person at any time. So I asked the postmaster how do I handle this. He said, "you are just going to have to chance it by running across the street to that bank over there,' pointing to a bank across the street. and changed your money into a certified cashiers check," so that's just what I did. Believe me I ran across the street making sure there weren't any M.P. s or S.P.s around and quickly converted it into a cashiers check. Why I thought I had to cash in those postal savings in Honolulu instead of just taking them back to the mainland and cashing them in there never entered my mind. Getting back to the ship 1 started packing all my belongings including a ship's bell we had supposedly surveyed and gotten rid of by tossing it over board and a very pistol and a boat compass off the S.S. Parada, the ship from which we had rescued the sailors. The day I got my orders to catch the ship back to S.F. I saw that it was going to be the U.S.S. Henderson AP1, the very same ship that I had taken over to the Islands when I came out here in 1940. What a blow, this must have been the slowest ship in the whole Navy, she had a speed of about 8 knots and all I could think of was that I would be eating lousy chow for about eight days going back to S.F. I climbed aboard her in Pearl Harbor wearing my dungarees with no rating showing on my sleeve. I immediately looked for the chiefs quarters and found their regular mess boy who was a sea/1c and told him that I was a sea/1c and could he use some help in the chief's mess quarters. He jumped at the chance to have some one help him, so I figured I was set for chow as the chief's had the best chow on most ship's which I was well aware of. He never questioned me on my rating so I got away with it, as no rated man was supposed to work as a galley slave. I figured the food was excellent and 1 also managed to get the look out watch at night during the time changes, so I managed to cut short the time on those watches where they jumped the time an hour as we came back over the time zones. It paid to have a little savvy on how to operate on a navy ship. We had some very shell shocked sailors on board and they never did like any of our humor when we would tell jokes or kid each other about our ships or what we had done while in the war zone. All this story telling was done while on lookout watch, you could tell your story over our sound powered head sets without being identified if some one took offense to what you were saying. Every once in awhile the Officer on Deck would get on the set and tell us to knock off the story telling and be serious about the lookout positions. Since I had very good night vision I would report anything that showed up on the water like those Japanese glass balls that fishermen used with their fishing nets. I can remember on two occasions where I spotted these glass balls and they were about the size of volley balls and maybe there were three or four of them sort of stuck together. What they really wanted was sighting of a submarine or a floating mine as we had no escort with us and it would have been a disaster if we did get hit by a torpedo or a mine, cause that old tub would have sunk in a few minutes. We finally arrived on the coast, in the early morning and every one was on deck as we could see Mount Tamalpais in the distance. When we cruised past the Farallons we could see that beautiful Golden Gate Bridge just ahead of us and everyone on board cheered as we passed underneath it. What a lovely feeling, to be home safe for awhile. As we sailed into the harbor, I could see Alcatraz Island and all the familiar land marks like Angel Island, Coit Tower and then the Ferry Building. I could even smell that delicious smell of roasting coffee wafting past my nose. While going down to my bunk to gather up my seabag and mattress gear, the P.A. came on loud and clear with this message, "all hands stand by for seabag inspection." This announcement startled me greatly as I had that compass and very pistol from the merchant ship PARADA and I had the ship's bell from the Tiger I was about to empty my seabag and leave this stuff behind when the P.A. came on again with another announcement, belay (cancel) that last announcement, baggage inspection will be for civilian passengers only! What a relief, I could still get my souvenirs home. I went back to the chiefs quarters and said good bye to the mess cook whom I had talked into letting me help with his mess and waiting on the chief's at meal time. We shook hands and said good bye to each other when he noticed that I had on second class crow rating (petty officer), this disturbed him greatly, that he was ordering a petty officer around and didn't know it. I laughed and told him that I knew he wouldn't have let me mess cook for the chiefs if he had known I was a second class petty officer. We parted as good friends and wished each other good luck. As we departed the ship we were told to assemble for transportation to Treasure Island via landing barges which I could see were LST barges. I had to laugh here I was safely in the states and going to get a ride on a landing barge to an Island without being shot at. Before we boarded the barge I happen to see the baggage tractor pulling a series of those baggage wagons that were so familiar around the Ferry Building, they were loaded with coffins that had been on board, this made me feel really sad as I remembered the poor guy who had be shot at that Alohoa Tower Army beer garden and I felt he could have been one of the unfortunates being shipped home. We had a quick ride over to Treasure Island and were assembled in a large hall where they announced that we would be there for three days while we were being processed and sent to our designated assignments. I thought hey, I'm not going to go through this rigamarole, I quickly found a pay phone near by, luckily there was one that wasn't in use, and called the Coast Guard District office in San Francisco to see if I could get off of Treasure Island and avoid all this baloney that they were trying to lay on me. A chief yeoman answered the phone and when I told him my name he exclaimed "Swede" how the hell are you and what can I do for you." Was I surprised to hear someone call me by my nick name here in the states; it made me feel as if the Coast Guard really cared for me! I told him where l was and what they were trying to do to me and he said, "Not to worry I'll have some one pick you up within the hour." Sure enough there was the truck ready to pick me up. Was I happy that I didn't have to put up with all that baloney on Treasure Island.   The driver had everything ready and all I had to do was toss my seabag on to the back of the truck and hop aboard for the ride to the district office in San Francisco. On the way over the driver told me we weren't going to the district office I knew but we would be going to the new receiving station at Bay and Powell St. I was told that it was the old Simmons Mattress factory and that we had taken it over for a receiving station. With my seabag I got out of the truck and checked in. I was given twenty days leave immediately, which I gladly accepted. I got an OK to leave my seabag there in storage until I could get transportation to carry it home to Mill Valley where my folks lived.

Chapter 40.

Marin County.

So I started out for home. My folks knew nothing about my coming home. After finding out that the Greyhound buses were not running because of some kind of dispute with the drivers I decided to hitchhike home. I found out there was no problem getting a ride while in uniform. A nice lady picked me up and away we went over the Golden Gate bridge into Marin County towards Mill Valley. I was taking in all the views I could and as we crested the hill after leaving the Waldo Tunnel I began to anticipate the view of Mt. Tamalpais and Richardson Bay. Just as we headed down the last mile off the Waldo grade I saw a very unfamiliar sight, some kind of housing construction in the small valley to the left of the highway, I exclaimed, "Who's building the chicken houses?" The lady driving laughed, and said, "We are, I'm involved with the project and the government is building those chicken houses for the Marin ship yard workers, if you look to the right you can see a ship yard where they are building victory ships for the war effort." What a surprise, there was this huge ship building project going on where the old mud flats used to be across from the American Distillery, which was located just across the road that leads to Sausalito. They even cut down a small hill just south of the marsh to fill in the land so that they could lay out a ship yard. The lady let me out right down town and it was only a short walk to my folks house on Cornelia Ave. Everyone was happy to see me. Home sure looked great but there was quite a bit of confusion as the folks had been in an automobile wreck and were just recovering from it. The car was in the shop and everyone one was taking it easy trying to heal as fast as they could. They were glad to see me and when I presented them with five cartoons of Lucky Strike Cigarettes, I was considered a war hero! After a 20 day leave I was glad to get back to the receiving station to find out what my new assignment was going to be. I should explain that being home was nice but all the guys I knew were gone or drafted and there were all kinds of restrictions on gasoline and food. It seemed that you had to have coupons for everything and I was not helping by using some one's civilian coupons, so I was better off going back to the protection and living quarters of the good old US Coast Guard (now Navy). I enjoyed my twenty days leave with folks but was anxious to get back to the receiving station to find out where I was going to be stationed. At the station the first thing they asked me was, "Where are your campaign ribbons and why haven't you got them on your uniform?" I said, "What ribbons, I don't know anything about this stuff?" They told me what ones to get at the PX right in the building which I did. I think they wanted all CG personnel to wear their ribbons because we never ever had much in the way of publicity on what we were doing in this great awful war. While in the PX I spotted a chronograph wrist watch, a Swiss model, that looked like something I could use in my work such as timing how fast my code speed was, etc so I bought it. After eating lunch in the mess hall I went back to the office and was told that my new assignment was going to be on the COMWESTSEAFRON Communications truck. I would be on subsistence and quarters (living &

housing) and the truck was kept in a garage near the Coast Guard Headquarters on Sansome Street. Boy, did this sound like good duty, even though once in awhile we would have to work in the communication office at Navy Headquarters. This job lasted about two months when the Warrant Officer in charge of NMC SF Radio (main radio station for this area) decided that he wanted the truck to be stationed at the site that the CG was building on Sweeny Ridge just above San Bruno. In fact the SF County Jail was located just below where our new barracks was being constructed. So we were sent to Sweeny Ridge to help build the new Communication Center and lay out all the antenna systems, and any thing else that would have to be done. In the mean time we were still attached to the Communications truck. My partner was a RM2/nd class by the name of Harold Schunard, who was married and was living in South San Francisco, he was unhappy because we were losing our subs and quarters. Sweeny Ridge was located in about the most miserable, wind torn, foggiest place in the world.

Chapter 41.

Back To Work.

The communication building was located right on the highest ridge and was built of concrete. Everything was first class, we were all put to work installing the new equipment. The barracks were built down below the ridge in sort of a sheltered area. We could see the SF. County jail located just about 300 yards below our barracks. In fact we built our horse shoe pit very close to their chain link fence, because there seemed to be less wind in this spot. The CG furnished a Jeep for the changing of the watches as it was a long way up the hill to the communications building. They also made room for our communications truck. It was a Mack Truck and had that great looking bull dog for a radiator ornament. There was only one thing wrong with the truck, the brass thought it would be prudent to install a governor on the gas pedal so that no matter hard you tried it would only go forty five miles per hour and that was only in the highest gear. In all the other gears it would govern the speed as if it were in high gear so that we couldn't get full power when going up steep hills in the lower gears. NMC S.F. Radio was designated official monitoring radio station for the ComWestSeaFron area with headquarters down town. My partner Harold and I got called to the downtown Naval headquarters for routine exercises and tests to see how well the truck was operating. We always had a Naval officer ride along who was in charge of the operation, I figured that the Admiral wanted this rig ready to go if there ever were an invasion or emergency. On one of our jaunts there was a cute Navy Lt. Wave riding with us and I got to talking to her, which irritated the officer in charge, because she was asking me about the Coast Guard and seemed interested in what we did. I had the feeling that I could have dated her but knowing the rules I didn't make any advances, as I could see that the officer was getting madder and madder, so I shut up and dropped the whole conversation. I think the reason we were on this test run was he wanted to get to know this cute wave officer! I never saw her again during my time on that truck.

On another trip Lt Cmdr Hosmer, USN, and a navy chief, a master sargent in the marines, Harold and I drove the truck to Mare Island to inspect some operating transmitters on the base. They were all riding in the back of the truck or van sitting in comfortable chairs and only Harold and I were up front. I was driving. When we came to the Mare Island entrance on Highway 37 a marine guard at the gate stopped us and started to give us a hard time, saying we couldn't enter the Mare Island Navy yard, yelling who do you think you are? All I did was let out a yell like, "Hey sarge can you come up front I got a problem?" The sargent came up front growling as they can when some one has yelled at them "what the hell is wrong with you marine we're going in or someone is going to be sorry?" I never saw a marine turn white so fast in my life especially when the sargent told him that the Coast Guard was doing a hell of a lot more than he was! It made me feel real good. We went into the yard and stopped at a transmitter building and went in to look at some new water cooled transmitters that just been put into service, they were the latest development in transmitters. They had 2000 watt water cooled tubes that were only about the size of a pint milk bottle. The petty officer in charge of the tranmitters showed us all around and we had a pretty good idea of what was going on in Naval communications. One thing that was established was the fact that we, at Sweeny Ridge could call Mare Island communications and use one of their transmitters if need be. All we had to do is request it and they would connect it to our keying system by land line and it was ours to use. If the navy wanted to use one of our transmitters they could request it and it would be put on their landline to use, since we had a transmitter that covered a wide range of frequencies. They did use this transmitter a few times when they had to use an odd frequency to work with. We all thought it was a worth while trip so on the way back I suggested that we stop for a beer in a tiny bar near Black Point on Highway 37. Every one thought it was a good idea, little did they know that I was friend of the owners! However we didn't linger too long and every one was back to his respective base in time for dinner.

Chapter 42.

Army Airforce Radar.

This time we got a call to drive up to the top of Mt. Tamalpais to see what was wrong with Air Force Radar installation. Lt Cmdr Hosmer told us this as we were driving across the Golden Gate bridge. He said they were getting some kind of interference on their radar scope and they thought we could identify where it was coming from. We drove through Mill Valley and then took the road that would take us all the way up to the radar site on the mountain. When we got there we were greeted

327

by the C.O., who happened to be an Army Airforce Captain. He greeted us like long lost cousins and proceeded to tell us about his problems with the radar. He lead us into the control room where the scopes were running showing what they could sweep. We could see that they had a problem with this interference. Being operators in communications we immediately recognized the interference as signals coming from the Navy low frequency high powered submarine channel. This transmission was at a very low frequency some where around 18 kilocycles or Herz. We told him the source and that he would have to filter the signal out because this was our long range submarine communication system. We also told him that it was possible that he had a loose connection or bad solder joint which acted like a detector and produced the problem on the radar screen. He thanked us for coming up and helping out with his problem and then invited us all to lunch. Lt Comdr Hosmer said it was fine with him so we all started out in the direction of the mess halls with the officers heading towards the officers mess and we all headed for the NCO mess hall. The CO seeing that we were headed for the NCO mess hall said no, "You guys are going to eat with us." We all looked at Lt Comdr Hosmer and he nodded his head with an OK sign so we all trouped over to the officers mess. Believe me, this is something that never happens in the CG or the Navy. We all sat down at the same table and I had an Airforce 2nd Lt ask me how I wanted my steaks cooked! Wow, I nearly fell out of my chair I was so shocked but I quickly recovered and told him I would like it medium rare. Then another shock came when I found out he was the server! After lunch we proceeded down the hill feeling pretty good because we were able to solve the Air Forces problem and had such a good lunch.

Nothing was mentioned about the officers mess or the people who worked as waiters but I sure bragged about it amongst my co-workers. I got the feeling that the Air Force was a more lenient type organization.

I remember one time driving up to Novato, where one of my high school buddies lived, thinking I could see him but found out he was working at the Marin ship yards so I turned around to go back to Mill Valley, stopping on my way back at an old time bar that was located at the Lucas Valley turn off. This place was one of the Hamilton Field Air Force hangouts or watering holes as we called them. I went in to get myself a cool beer and found the place loaded with Air Force pilots all sitting at the bar. I leaned up against the bar near the end of the bar and ordered a Lucky beer and started to drink it standing up when one of the young pilots exclaimed, "Hey guys here is a guy who has seen actual war duty (as he recognized my campaign ribbons}, we can't have him standing up while none of us has seen anything but training camps and fresh California air." They insisted on me sitting down and when they heard that I had gone through the Pearl Harbor disaster they started buying me drinks. Of course they wanted to hear my story which I told rather reluctantly, you see I really had thought about how hard it was to tell a story like that, it was so awe some. However, they seemed to like what I told them and I managed to get out of there without too much booze. Later on I did contact my friend who was working at the ship yard and found out he was being drafted in about three months. He eventually ended up in the Army and found himself in the middle of the Battle of the Bulge. He managed to survive his Army duty and returned to Novato after the war ended.

George C. Larsen

During this time my best friend Scott came through S.F. on his new assignment as navigator on the Navy transport the Gen. Randal a large two stack twenty thousand ton ship. We went on a pretty good spree in down town S.F. and he stayed over night at my folks place and went back to the ship the next day as he had the duty. We saw each other at different times as it seemed that we would end up in the same area as I for just enough time to throw a good party. In our early days over in Hawaii we always talked about how we were going to rent an apartment in S.F. and all we would have in our refrigerator would be beer, nothing else! As you can guess it never happened but we always managed to go on a little spree and consume a lot of beer. It did look a little strange to see us going from bar to bar in down town San Francisco, especially in the fancy bars like the top of the Mark and the Sir Francis Drake Hotel. Nothing was ever mentioned about the difference in our ratings, as most of the people in uniforms had never gotten out of the states and they could see by our ribbons that there was a sort of a sort of a bond between us that they didn't have. We never talked about what we did to any one. We also communicated by letters to each other so we could keep in contact, although he had better facilities to find out where I was than I did for him. I don't know how he found out where I was at times but he always seemed to turn up where I least expected him.

Around September 1943 I got a call from Jim Elliot the Motor Machinist off the Tiger. He was going to fire damage control and diving class on Treasure Island. He said he thought he would go into salvage work, especially in the Red Sea and around the Suez Canal area. He came over to the house and we talk about the times we had on the Tiger Maru, of course this was when I also had my liberty from NMC.   About that time another acquaintance from the Navy cruiser St Louis came into Mare Island. His ship was in for repairs, so he called and came over to visit with my whole family, his name was Kirby Jones and his rating was gunner's mate 1st class. I didn't know it at the time but he had taken a liking to one of my sisters and came to the house often before I ever got back from the Islands. When he found out that I too had been at Pearl during the bombing we became fast friends. We exchanged stories on where we were and what we had to do during the raid and afterwards.

Being a gunners mate he told me that they had taken all their firing pins out of their heavy guns like the ones in his turret which had twin 5 inch 38 cal cannons that were mostly anti-aircraft guns and had taken them over to the navy machine shop to be machined. When the bombing started he had to run over to the machine shop to get the firing pins.

They did manage to get the pins back in time to fire at the incoming planes especially the second time they came over on the second raid at around ten o'clock that morning.

Chapter 43.

Man Overboard!

Kirby and I went on some pretty good libertys. He invited me to their ships dance at the Palace Hotel and we had a great time. The next time I saw him he called me from Mare Island and said they had just gotten in but he couldn't get any liberty because some sailors had shoved an officer over the side just as they were coming up to the Golden Gate and another ship following them spotted the officer in the drink and they picked him up. He said the officer had them all detained so that he could see if he recognized any one who had been in the party that shoved him over the side. Kirby told me he was a rotten officer and was mean and nasty. He said it was to bad that he was spotted in the water but maybe he would straighten up after he realized how the enlisted men felt about him. After two days the man gave up on trying to identify who pushed him over the side at midnight and they had to let everyone go on liberty, or leave after that. That time Kirby brought two of his buddies with him and my folks accommodated them all overnight. One guy was slightly mad at me when I woke him up since I had to yell really, "hit the deck you swabs", he felt I was too bossy! After that Kirby came over by him self. He would called his mother from our house to his in Norfolk, Virginia. My folks were glad to let him, figuring that this was their way of contributing to the war effort. At the time I was going with a young Catholic girl from San Bruno, so I took Kirby along with me one day, not knowing that this gals father didn't like enlisted men and he seemed annoyed when I brought along a lowly sailor. I got the impression that he thought we were lowering his life style by being present in his home. I told him how Kirby had just finished fighting in the South Pacific around Guadalcanal and the Solomon Islands. This didn't soften him up at all. At the time my girl friend was talking about getting married but after that session with her father I sort of cooled off on that idea. A couple of hours with them that day was all I could stand. We took off for San Francisco and hit all the top bars in town for a good time. Kirby returned to his ship and I went back to the station up on windy hill.

On the hill one of my duties was monitoring all Navy transmitters in the area including Oahu. One night I found a transmitter working on the wrong frequency, not by much but according to my frequency meter instrument it was slightly off by a few cycles, so I logged it and went on with other duties. Much to my surprise, a civilian, from Washington D.C. came to the station to interview me. First of all he wanted to see how I checked the frequency readings of the transmitters, which I demonstrated for him, then he told me he was going to go to Oahu and check out that transmitter. I never knew what his position in the Navy was but I figured he wanted to get some time in a war zone. I didn't think that little shift in frequency was that serious.

Chapter 44.

A Promotion & Action!!

Our yeoman, a chief who had been on the Tiger with me, was questioned by the officer in charge as to why I was only second class? Charlie Noble, the yeoman, told him, "Out in the Pacific no one got promoted because there just weren't any openings for promotions. Back in the states there were plenty of openings for promotions." Being a mustang officer, (up through the enlisted mens rank), this CO decided right then and there that I should have the first class rating. This did great things to my pay check which certainly helped.

The operation was a bit different than what we did on Oahu, here again we had to take an inner oath swearing that we would never discuss what we were doing at this facility. Since the war is over I can tell you about this duty. Two of us were put on a monitor schedule copying messages that were being sent to German Wolf Pack submarine groups. This was a highly elaborate technical system that the Germans had developed. The system was very clever. They put low powered signals in the middle of our high powered shore station transmitting signals and sent their instructions and directions to their Wolf Packs all in German encrypted code. We had some very sensitive receivers with crystal selectivity abilities where we could tune into their low powered transmissions and copy the whole message. Since there were two of us copying the stuff both copies went into Navy intelligence and they could break down the messages even though some times we had different letters when copying the messages. The German station were somewhere in Central and South America. They must have been pretty damn effective because one of my watch partners whom I liked very much got orders to go under cover in search of these clandestine stations. Before he left he sold me all of his guns, a 30 30 saddle rifle, a 12 gage shot gun and a 22 rifle. He was married and didn't want his wife to be responsible for this gear and beside he wanted her to have a little extra cash while he was gone on this mission. I paid him around a hundred dollars for the guns, which was a pretty good price for that time. I never heard if they had successful mission or not, I had left the station before that mission was completed.

One night while on a regular watch where I was the supervisor I heard a very erratic signal coming in on the emergency frequency 500 kcs or Herz, I had a very green operator on this channel so I said to him, "Watch out that sounds like a very nervous hand on the key and he might be in trouble." Just as I said that the signal sort of straighten out and sounded like an SOS. Sure enough it was an SOS and this ship had run aground out on the Farralone Islands and was sinking fast. We turned this one in very fast to headquarters so that they could act on it quickly. We heard later that the crew and passengers all got ashore on the Island safely with no lives lost but every thing else went down with the ship. On my next liberty to Mill Valley I met a young sailor who had been on that ship as a passenger and he was telling me all about the sinking saying that was the third ship he had been on that sank within the last three months. He explained that the first one was a converted four stack destroyer from World War one, that they had made it into an attack transport by eliminating two boiler rooms which also eliminated two of the smoke stacks. This made room for carrying attack troops for invasion forces when needed. He told me it was a Coast Guard manned ship with a few Naval personnel like him self to fill the complement up to a fully manned crew. He then told me how they were sunk. It seems that they spotted a Naval aviator at night with one of those life ring lights that light up when you hit the water. After spotting the raft or ring they proceeded carefully towards the pilot because they were very close to Tulaugi Island which was held by the Japanese at the time. Just as they pulled up to the pilot they could see that the pilot was dead because there was no movement in the ring. Before anyone knew what was happening a shore battery opened up on them and made a direct hit right in the middle of the ship with more than one shell. It was then that everyone realized the Japanese had a couple of cannons or shore batteries trained on the ring and that they had set up a trap that their ship fell into. He said that they had to abandon ship quickly. They got away from the ship as quickly as they could, the boatswain in charge of their life boat asked him to get the ID tags off of a poor sailor who's whole chest had been ripped open. He said it was awful because he had to feel around in all that blood trying to find the tags which he finally found and removed from the sailor. In the mean time they discovered that the life boat was filling up with water and panic set in with every able bodied person bailing for the rest of the night. In the early morning they discovered that no one had put the plugs in the bottom of the life boat and that was the cause of all of the water coming in! They finally got picked up by another ship and ended up on the Helena, a cruiser. It didn't take to long and the Helena was shot up either by torpedoes or shell and it sank promptly. So all in all he survived three sinkings in about three months or less. He did say he had a lot of respect for the Coast Guard after doing duty on that destroyer. I was amazed at how calmly he reacted to three sinkings, I attributed it to his age; he was all of 18 years old. Several of us had discussed this phenomenon and came to the conclusion that any one over the age of 35 did not perform as well as younger men in any war front or battle. However that was only our opinion as we had observed several breakdowns in older persons during the Dec 7th raid especially a day or two afterwards when the bombing took its toll and you could see and feel the end result.

Chapter 45.

Port Chicago.

We were on stand by duty on the night of July 17th, 1944, we were lounging around the barracks watching a movie or playing ping pong when we felt a heavy rush of air and a very loud rumble. It was big enough for everyone to stop what they were doing and speculate on what it was or what caused this disturbance. About ten minutes later I got a phone call from the district office down town asking me to bring the communication truck down to Third and Market street where the OD officer from the district office would meet the truck and we were going to head for some place in the east bay. I got my partner for the night and we were driven up the hill to the ComWesSeaFron communications truck and started out for downtown S.F. We picked up the officer at third and Market and headed for the Oakland Bay Bridge's truck lanes which were right along side the railway tracks that ran on the lower deck. The officer wanted us to go as fast as we could go, the only problem was that damn governor on the throttle, really attached to the carborator, wouldn't let us go over 45 miles per hour no matter how hard we tried. I also complained about the fact that we didn't have a red light and sirens to get us to any scene without delays by slow poke drivers who wouldn't give way on the freeway. The officer, told us that there had been an explosion at Port Chicago and we were to cover the scene and report in detail all the things that went on there. He also wanted to know if I knew how to get there? I had a pretty good idea because I knew it was near Pittsburgh, California. We arrived around midnight and I parked in the middle of the town and began to run up all our antenna systems. I ran up our vertical antennas and then began to string up our long wire airplane antenna if we had to use our regular high frequency transmitters. We found out that we couldn't raise our local station for some reason but we could talk or transmit to our Seattle station so we started sending everything to our sister station in Seattle who in turn relayed it to our local station in San Francisco. In putting up the long wire antenna I had to go into an upstairs apartment and hang out the front window to tie up the end of the wire. While entering the apt. I found that the linoleum on the floor had risen to about four feet in the air and I had to push it down as I walked across the floor to the window. When I got near the window I noticed that there was a baby crib sitting near the window and that the glass in the window was completely blown away and that most of it was in the baby crib, lucky there was no baby in the crib at that time.

We talked to the only survivor, from all of the men involved in the loading of that lethal cargo. He told us that two ammunition ships had blown up in the harbor and the only reason he was alive is because he decided to call his wife on the phone and he had to go into Port Chicago to do so. It was while he was phoning that the two ships blew up. They had been loading high explosive ammunition on one of the ships and were just finishing up and he was getting ready to go to sea when he decided to tell his wife. Another person told me that one of the ships anchors fell to the ground in the middle of the downtown area. These anchors weigh about two or three tons. There were some estimates that anchor was hurled at least a half of a mile. Most of the store fronts in town had all their glass windows broken. One fellow came along and offered us a swig of booze that he had grabbed out of a store window that had broken out. Of course we turned him down. We didn't need to go down to the harbor to look at the damage as there wasn't much left to see, even the Coast Guard picket boat had disappeared with all hands lost. I heard that there were at least 320 lives lost on that explosion. There was a Coast Guard picket boat patrolling the area on the out side location from the ships. It completely vanished in the explosion. My folks even felt the shock waves in Mill Valley and they have several hills to block it out. We returned to our base in the early morning and we were all thankful that we didn't have ammunition ship duty.

Chapter 46.

Testing.

After that mishap the people in charge decided to see how well our communications would work up around Mendocino Country, which is about 150 miles from San Francisco. We drove up freeway US 101 to the turn off to Booneville and the Coast. We got there late in the evening and it started raining. They wanted to try the phone frequencies so I got out of the truck to run up one of the vertical antennas. As I stepped to the ground and started pushing the vertical antenna poles up by hand felt something crawl up my pants leg on the inside. I knew it was some kind of bug and it seemed pretty big so I reached down where I felt it moving and grabbed my pants leg material and began squeezing it real hard as I knew I had the thing in the folds of my pants, I could felt it struggling as I kept squeezing, I then rolled up my pants leg to the point where I could dump it out on the ground. In the mean time the guys in the truck are all wondering what the hell was wrong with me dancing around out in the rain like a lunatic. Looking at this big bug on the ground I saw that it was one of those awful looking potato bugs, that look as if they have a heavy armored head gear. That bug must have been running around looking for some place to hide when it started raining. We worked with our station to every one's satisfaction and headed back home, mission accomplished. The only casualty was a bug!

Back at the station I went back to my old routine of guarding the emergency frequencies. It must have been about 11 PM PDT when I picked up a very weak signal sending an SSS distress call, he used the standard NUMS7 call to disguise who he was and I believe that the seven meant he was in the South Pacific. I cranked up our big low freq transmitter on the same frequency and told him to go ahead with his SSS. He came right back to me and said I'm shifting up to 36, I said OK (go ahead), I yelled to one of the other operators to help me find him on 36 meters which we did right away. He sent a plain language message to us that a Submarine had been trailing him for about two or three hours but hadn't been able to catch up to him yet, then he gave us his position in longitude and latitude which enable us to find his position instantly. Were we surprised that he was about 800 miles south of Tahiti! Our sister station at Half Moon Bay, the old

McKay commercial station called us on the teletype and said he didn't hear a thing until we answered the call. We were all amazed that we could hear or pick up this 500 kcs or 600 meters signal from that far away. We also noticed that a message left the big NPG Naval transmitter going to the Tahiti Naval Base about this sub sighting and that it went in coded language. I often wondered about sending that message because if the Japanese were copying all this stuff it would have given them an opening into breaking some of our coded messages. But lucky for us it never happened. The operator signed off saying I guess I should have encoded this message but I didn't have time to do it.

In the fall of 1944 we began to pick up weak SOS signals but couldn't pin down who was sending them or where they came from. We finally picked up some of the signals on our new direction finder that had a built in scope. We noticed that they seem to be coming from some where on the water front according to our direction finder. So we thought some body was trying to distract us. We soon discovered that it was a testing station checking out the emergency transmitters that were built for the life rafts on troop transports, the signals had been leaking out due to a faulty dummy load system that they were using. It was quickly corrected and we had no more trouble from that source.

Around this time I got a call from one of my old summer time friends who hung out in our neighborhood every year. He told me he had just completed pilot training flying a B17 fortress. He said he would be going over seas soon, so I congratulated him on his commission. His brother was a fighter pilot and had been shot down several times in the Mediterranean theater and was a full colonel doing war bond tours in the states. About two months later I heard from his aunt that the bomber pilot had been shot down in a raid over Germany and was never found. About this time one of the chiefs from the MacKay station told me that he was being transferred to a new transport troop ship and he was looking for operators and thought that I should be one of those guys to go on it. Since I never volunteer for any thing I thought he probably would get me on that ship. I was getting tired of this shore duty anyway. I think it was early in the spring when we had a big storm come in from the Pacific. When I went on watch I had to struggle out of the van to the front door of the operations building. As I entered I noticed the anemometer was really spinning around, so I ran over to the area where the meter was located just to see how strong the wind was blowing. Much to my surprise the meter that took the readings went only to seventy five miles per hour and the indicator was pegged at that reading. I think that the real speed of the wind was around a hundred miles an hour. It did a lot of damage around the area like blowing down trees and utility poles and wires. A rumor spread around the barracks one Friday night that we were going to have an inspection of the facilities by an admiral, so we should be ready for a general uniform inspection also. The C.O. said no tailor made uniforms were to be worn on this inspection tour. So I immediately dug out my original G.I. issue Blues that I acquired when in boot camp. This uniform was designed before World War One. The middy had a draw string to tighten up around your waist so that the surplus length of the blouse would hang down to the right length around the waist and the pants had pure stove pipe legs with a string laced split in the back to accommodate various sizes. Needless to say, the C.O. had a fit when he saw me line up for the inspection in this garb but he couldn't say anything about it since he had issued that order, no tailor mades. We passed muster and everyone was happy, even the Admiral.

Right near our living quarters was a large field of artichokes that belonged to a farm just below our place. Since most of the crew had never heard of this plant I decided to swipe a few to cook and show them what a delicacy they were. After cooking them I gave each person one and told them to either use mayonnaise or butter to dip the leaves in and scrape off the meat with their teeth, explaining that was the way we natives ate this morsel. When I started to show them exactly how to do it a artichoke worm became exposed in my artichoke. Everyone was staring at my plate and remarking things, like aren't you going to eat that worm? So just to be smart I dipped the worm in mayo and swallowed it, it was the color of the artichoke and was pure artichoke as far as I could tell. The whole gang just about had conniptions over the fact that I had swallowed the worm and let me know that they thought I was crazy. I acted like that was an every day occurrence with me and casually let them know it was nothing to get excited about. The next night at dinner everyone was at the table waiting for me to sit down when the mess cook came in with a plate covered over with a lid and placed it in front of me. Everyone was looking at me with high expectations, so I lifted the lid to see what was under there, I figured it would be something gross and sure enough they had dug up about a dozen earth worms and put them on a plate expecting me to eat them. Well I had to laugh because it was such a good stunt to pull on me but as you can guess I never ate the worms. Of course they all needled me because I wouldn't touch the nasty critters.

One last thing about this assignment, for entertainment we pitched horse shoes and played ping pong. All of us who participated in these activities got very good at them. In fact we could slam the ping pong ball as hard as any of the professional players of that time, we played at it so much. On the horse shoe pitching we never got too good at because it was a day time event and we had to hike down the hill to get to the horse shoe pits. The other entertainment was 16 millimeter movies that were shown when ever we could get a decent movie. One movie we enjoyed was a navy propaganda movie called "Fighting Lady," a movie of a large carrier ship like the Enterprise making bombing runs on Guam and surrounding Islands. What was unusual about this picture was the fact they did the whole thing in color. They must have gone to a great expense to mount camera's in those bombers and fighter planes, especially using color film.

Well the day finally came, when I got orders saying I was to transfer to Bay and Powell then on to a new ship that was being commissioned that week at the Oakland Army Depot. The name of the ship was the USS A.W. Greely, A.P.141. So the first thing they wanted to do was give me a new Booster Shot. The pharmacist mate who was giving the shot complained that he couldn't get through my tough skin to give me the shot, I complained that the needle was not sharp enough. He finally poked around and got through and gave me my booster shot. After that I gathered up all my gear and started out for Bay and Powell, the receiving station, to be processed for the transfer to the troop ship. When I got there they said I had to wait until the next day before going to the ship. I complained that the ship was being commissioned that day and I was supposed to be on board. That didn't phase anyone at the receiving station so I missed being a plank owner (original crew member) by one day. Some how this was very important to me but no body else thought so. While waiting around the barracks I ran into a chap who looked as if he needed a friend. He was in dungarees and he started talking to me and I listened to his story. It seems that he missed his ship on purpose out of San Diego and got caught soon after that as he went back to his bride of a few weeks and was picked up there by the shore patrol. They gave him six months in the brig and broke him down to seaman 2nd class. He then told me the only clothes he had were what he was wearing and that he couldn't get any thing till he got enough money to buy clothes at small stores. He was out of the brig and waiting for an assignment. I remember that I had a set of old liberty type uniforms so I offered them to him. All he had to do was take the first class crow off the sleeve and he could have them. He was so happy to get something to wear it made me feel as if I had done some thing right for a change. It took me two more days before I got over to the ship which was tied up at the Oakland Army Supply Dock which was quite near the Oakland Bridge toll booths but across the water about a 100 yards or so. I forgot how I got there but the first day I got on board I got a phone call from Scott Berryman, who wanted me to go on liberty with him. I still don't know how he found out where I was but I managed to get a liberty pass and met him at the gang way of the ship and we had a ball in downtown S.F. I never knew whether his ship was in port or whether he was on leave visiting his folks. Anyhow, I went back to the ship that night and I didn't see Scott till the end of the June on the East Coast.

Chapter 47.

Back to Sea Duty.

With the crew all aboard we set sail for San Francisco tying up at pier 41, where they had a degaussing check system to see if our degaussing system (an anti-magnetic devise) was working O.K. we soon found out that there was a great bar (cocktail) across road and across some of the waterfront rail tracks, so we made that our official hangout. The pier housing had a huge stack of Army office equipment inside and we thought it would be great if we could get our hands on one of

365

their nice desks and a chair. The Army Officer in charge said, "No way", of course we never got the desk but we threw a scare into him when we asked him if he knew what a Midnight Requisition was? (Take an object with out an order) While we were tied up there we had a visitors day for family or other military personnel. I happened to be in charge of one of the day watches in the radio shack and I was getting acquainted with the group who would be working with me. I had to entertain the military people who would wander into the radio shack. A group from Treasure Island Naval base came aboard and with them were several Navy Waves wearing 2nd and 1st class radio ratings. One of my third class men was copying the NPG Fox sked and one of the Waves asked if she could sit in and copy the messages for a while. I said fine, since we were only practicing at the time. Well, you couldn't have surprised me more, when this young wave sat down and began copying NPG and talking to us at the same time. This stuff was coming in at 20 words a minute and in code and she was copying it about two groups behind and talking to us at the same time. After she finished and the next one did the same thing I laughingly asked them if they wanted a transfer to our ship. They both said they wished they could but we all knew at the time it couldn't happen but wished it could be. They told me that they both worked for Western Union telegraph and could copy around 90 words a minute, which I could believe. While we were in the degaussing test area we discovered something was wrong with power plant to the turbines that turned the twenty seven ft diameter propellor and that we would have to go to Hunters Point Navy Yard to get it fixed. In the meantime, the chief radio man who asked for me to come aboard informed me that he had become a father that day. We ran over to the little bar a had drink in celebration of his fatherhood. The next day I was checking our spare tube inventory and found out that we didn't have any tubes at all, so the Warrant Officer in charge of the communications dept. decided that I had better go to Mare Island and get a bunch of spare tubes as we had no idea were we would be going in the future. Since I had already experienced not having a spare part in a strange place where there was no chance of ever getting a thing such as a tube or a capacitor etc. I was told to get at least one tube of every kind that we used so I made up a list of all the tubes we had in use and hoped that I could find them all. The next day I called the Navy transportation department and got a ride to Mare Island in a government car, a four door sedan with a civilian driver. There were three other people in the car all going to Mare Island for other reasons, they were all officers. When we got there I trotted around to all the supply warehouses and got what I wanted. I then had to go to a Naval office to get a release for all of the tubes that I had gotten. The first office I went too had a Lt. Commander who told me I had to go to another office and get a signature before he could release the tubes. At the second place I was told that I had to get a signature from another office, so back into the car I went looking for this other place. In the meantime the other passengers, all officers, were chomping at the bit to get back to S.F. as it was getting close to four o'clock, cocktail time. I was getting desperate myself wondering if I was ever going to get a release for my package as I knew those marines at the gate would think that I had stolen this stuff and I'd be delayed that much more. I even told these people the ship was leaving in the morning and I had to have these tube on board the ship. The last place I was sent to, was the very first place that I came to in the beginning, I faced the same Lt. Comdr!! I slammed down my package a yelled at the top of my voice, "What the hell is going on, I want this stuff released so that I can leave this Island," and lo and behold he grabbed my papers and signed the release. I'll never know why they gave me such a run around. We made it back to the city by about five PM so everyone was happy.

The next morning we left the pier and headed for Hunters Point Naval yard for our repair job on the engine. It had something to do with the controls. It took several days for this job because they had to wait for a part to show up so I had a chance to go home for an over night stay. I told the folks that we were going on a shake down cruise for about two weeks and that I would see them when we came back. My mother exclaimed, "That's nice" while she was doing a washing and listening to a soap opera, Ma Perkins, sponsered by Oxydol Soap Co. I said, "Ma are you listening to me?" just as some fiend was going to push Ma Perkins over a cliff just above her lumber yard. I said, "How could you listen to such tripe." She laughed and we kissed good bye and I left for the ship. We left Hunters Point and headed out to sea, with several of our electrical circuits fouled up, which we traced out and fixed. Of course we blamed those shipyard workers, however they may have only followed the blue prints that were given to them to work with. We headed south after leaving the Golden Gate when I was told that I needed a booster shot along with a whole bunch of other things. I protested that I had just gotten my booster shots at the receiving station but they said your medical records didn't come on board so we have to make sure that you have one, so I got another booster tetanus shot along with some other nasty looking immunization shots, one of them was for yellow fever, which gave me a hint that maybe we weren't on a shakedown cruise that would end up in S.F. again! The next day we arrived at an area next to the Channel Islands and the Navy was going to check out our ability to fire all our surface guns and our antiaircraft guns, along with seeing how our communications and loran and radar equipment was handled. The Channel Islands are located west of the Santa Barbara Channel. I happened to have the morning watch from 0800 to 1200 and saw that a bunch of Naval officers were coming aboard. We had a Lt. monitoring everything we did. We were told to operate with a shore station that they had going some place near Santa Barbara. His station called us on a given frequency and said they had a message for us. Since I was supervisor of the watch I told my watch stander on that frequency to challenge that station with our recognition code to see if he was legitimate, this confused the operator at the shore station, so the Lt observer said, "that's OK go ahead and eccept the message." I said, "no way," "This may be an enemy station" playing out the roll of a real operations." The Lt got very mad but we didn't ever answer the station and I told him that I had enough experience in the Pacific to know that you don't answer anyone or accept calls if the recognition signals isn't given. He left the radio shack mad as hell but I never saw him or heard anymore about our part in the exercise. The next thing that happened was they sent out a large gas driven drone airplane with a wing span of about twelve feet. It flew over the center of the ship and a dozen 20 millimeter cannons began firing at it. It must have flown over at about 1000 feet but didn't make it past the ship as it was torn to shreds and even the motor was shot out of the body. The next thing I heard was, was the question, "why did you shoot our drone down, they cost about 12,000 dollars, we didn't want it shot up like that!". I thought what kind of people are we dealing with.

The next thing that happened was the 40 millimeter cannons began firing at a target sleeve, I don't know how well they did but the noise was ear shattering. Then we began to fire our five inch thirty eight cannons at a target about 1000 yards away, all by radar fire control. We were the first ship in line to fire at the target as there were two Navy transport following us doing all the same things. Our first shot caught the top of a wave quite near the target that was being towed by a Navy tug and the shell skipped over the target just nicking the top as it went past. The next eleven shots went right through the bulls eye almost but we considered them direct hits. What impressed me most was the fact that the Navy transports never ever hit the target as we could see all of the shooting because we were still within sight of the target during the whole exercise. When I inquired about the reason for their missing the target, I was told that they were using the regular old fire control method not the radar method. By chow time in the evening we headed on to San Pedro where we were going to pick up some Army troops and a contingent of Red Cross workers, so the rumor went. Where we were going was anybody's guess.

We entered San Pedro Harbor and tied up for the night. The next day the Captain, a real Captain Steadman, with four gold stripes on his sleeve, informed us that there would visitors coming aboard. Apparently he had a lot of friends in the movie business, as the radio shack began to fill up with visitors who were well dressed and the women wore fancy clothes and they all seemed interested in what we were doing. I think one of the big Hollywood producers was in the shack with us because I heard him discussing his big orchid house that he was building and that he had about 500 plants and he really enjoyed this hobby. I remember reading about some producer with this kind of a hobby so I assumed that maybe this was the same guy. His lady friend kept questioning me about where we were going after we left San Pedro, I knew that she was just trying to see if we knew because I think she already knew, so I said, "I think we are going to India or some hot climate, I base my opinion by what I saw coming aboard in supplies and by the shots they had given us at the start of the trip down to here." She gave me a funny look, I thought that maybe I had hit the right place in my guess. That afternoon they gave us liberty and I took off for Long Beach cause I heard that they had a dance hall out on the water there. Maybe I could find some nice gal to date. I did find a girl who would dance with me even though I am a lousy dancer. When it was time to go home she asked me if I wanted to ride home with them. I didn't ask where but said I'd like to go along, asking at the time who else was there she said a girl and her boy friend and then the guy that brought her to the dance. She introduced me to the guy and we all hopped into his car. I found out we were going to Maywood a nice part of Los Angeles. I sat in back with the girl friend and her partner and the girl that asked me to ride home with them sat in front with the guy who had driven her to the dance. I noticed that he was a little mad about something and he started to drive faster and faster. It was about one o'clock in the morning by now and I was getting a little nervous about this fellow's driving. When he hit seventy miles a hour on this two lane road I said, "Stop the car!" "I'm not riding in this guy's car" and started to get out when he finally came to a stop. At that point the girl in the front seat got out and the other's followed me out to the side of the road. The guy drove off burning rubber and here we all were out in the country and I had no idea where we were. The next car coming down the road looked as if it were slowing down so I threw out my thumb and what do you know, they stopped. I explained that we just got out of a crazy drivers car and could they give us a lift to Maywood. The driver said. "Sure hop in we'll take you guys there." We got in when I noticed that it was a great big Cadillac and the four of us sat in the back seat easily. We got to Maywood and I escorted the girl whom I danced with to her house and talked to her for awhile. I said, "I've got to get back to my ship in San Pedro Harbor, how long will it take me if I get a good ride?" She didn't know but she told me what road to go down to get back to San Pedro. There wasn't a car on the road when I started back, mainly because it was around two thirty in the morning. I started worrying about getting back to the ship before eight AM. It was getting close to five AM and I was hiking down the rode thinking that at least I should be getting closer by walking. Finally a milk truck came by and picked me up. The driver asked me where I was headed for and I told him. He said that was right on his way so he would drop me off right at the gate to the piers. I got back to the ship about fifteen minutes to eight in time for muster call and a cup of coffee. The girl wanted me to come back and visit and maybe go to that famous dance band pavilion located in Maywood. The big bands like Glen Miller and Gene Krupa played there many time, I used to listen to them every Friday and Saturday night. So I got liberty again and took the big Red Train from Long Beach to the L.A. train station where she said she would meet me. When I got to the train station who should be with but her father. He drove us to the Pavilion and left us on our own. He was a very nice guy and he didn't seem to be too worried about me after he met me. We had a nice time at the dance and before it was over I ran into one of my old ship mates off of the

Tiger Maru, Orvile Delaney, who had his new wife with him so we talked about what we were doing and we would write or whatever when we had a chance. I told him what ship I was on and I thought we would get together after the war if it was possible. I took my girl friend back home and gave her a big good night kiss and took off for the ship. I got back early this time and it was a good thing because we were going to leave port soon and I didn't want to miss the ship because the penalty was pretty heavy if you did, remembering what happened to that poor sailor to whom I gave the uniforn. When I got back to the ship I saw that we had a full boat load of Army personnel. I looked at the work assignment sheet and saw that I caught the 2000 to 0200 watch. I had three operators working for me copying the fox schedule, monitoring the commercial band and one guy on the high frequency band or some times the TBS transceiver if needed. I took to copying the news from a high frequence station run by the associated press or Reuters or what ever station I could get. It was the only plain language code on the air at that time. Everything else was in code whether it was an Allied station or one of our enemy stations. One of the first important news stories I copied was the one giving notice that F.D. Roosevelt our president had died, that was on April 12th 1945. We were about four or five days out at sea at the time. During the trip we held many types of drills to keep every one sharp on what they were supposed to be doing. On one of the day time drills, general quarters, I had to man the emergency radio room which was down one deck from the main radio shack. I had one other man with me and we were manning our station when the executive officer Lt Comdr.R.S. Tewksbury burst into the radio room and the boatswain mate yelled attention! We both looked at them and never moved as we both were wearing our headsets and tuning in the stations that we were going to cover. The executive officer yelled, "Stand up at attention," we both struggled to our feet and I said "sir we are on watch manning our station we can't come to attention and do our job at the same time." He turned red in the face and did an about face and left the emergency radio room. We never heard another word about this from any one.

After about a week of traveling we could notice the change in temperature. It was getting warmer each day as we sailed closer to the equator. I knew I was in trouble because I had missed the crossing of the equator in 1940 when I got transferred off the Roger B Taney just as she was going to do a supply run to the Line Islands. All the guys who were Shellbacks (people who have crossed the equator) were waiting to get all of us Poly Wogs (those who haven't) One of the

Shellbacks was Rebel Allen, the chief who got me on the ship. Boy, what a beating we took as we crossed the line. Rebel gave me a haircut called the southern cross, which was a 2 inch cut down to the scalp from the front to the back and then another two inch cut from ear to ear. Then they smeared us with grease and pieces of shredded rope and threw us in a hand made pool of dirty water [salt], the pool was made out of heavy canvas and timbers. Where they got the material for all of this I'll never know but all in all it was exciting and fun. After cleaning up with a salt water shower I went to the barber shop the next day and had all my hair clipped off so that it would come in evenly as time would allow. On April 24 we crossed the international date line. That was the day I picked up a local military radio broadcast station that was out of Noumea, New Caladonia. I fed that program through the ships PA system for all those who wished to hear it. We usually fed music via the large electric transcriptions at the speed of 18 rpm on a turn table that was installed in the radio room. We could also use a microphone to make little announcements but no one felt like doing that so we left that part alone. Just when I thought I couldn't stand my uncleanliness the ship ran into a tropical squall were the rain came down so hard that deck was almost ankle deep with fresh water. I quickly got some soap and took a shower right out on deck with only my shorts on. Even though we had about 500 Red Cross girls on board I didn't care. They were all inside anyway. During the trip I had a contingent of army radio operators come into the radio shack to see how we operated. After quizzing them I found out that they were going to set up a communication line across the hump (mountains) from India to China. This confirmed my observation that we were going to India. We let these guys in anytime because they knew how to behave in a radio shack. We discussed the problems they were going to have and we all wondered when this damn war was going to end. Harry Truman was our president now and we didn't know who was vice president but we all wondered how Truman would act in trying to end this war. During the afternoon I would sit under a boom for shade and read a novel. This one day I didn't notice that I was sitting so that the sun crossed my legs above my knees up to the bottom of my cut off jeans. I only read for about an hour when I noticed that my legs were feeling kind of warm. I looked at my legs and they were turning red so I thought I had better get out of the sun, which I did. I went to my bunk and tossed the book on it and then took a look at my legs. Did I get a surprise, I could see a red glow in the dark from the burn I got from just that short stay in the tropical sun. I heard that we were getting close to Melbourne Australia.

It was early afternoon and we turned into the channel going to that port. As we were coming around the breakwater there was a girl semaphoring the ship with hand signals trying to arrange a date with anyone. Since I could read semaphore I got a big charge out of reading her request. Apparently some one on the bridge was answering her because I read "OK I'll meet you at the dock." My watch happen to have the liberty that night so we immediately ran down and took fresh water showers and got ready for liberty. Boy, was it great to walk on land again even though I was rolling a little bit as if I was still at sea. A couple of us found a bar with a whole bunch of old guys sipping beer. So the first thing I did was buy every one at the bar a drink, I think it cost me about 2 dollars but it put us on the good side of everybody there. The beer was really good. I left the bar to see what else could be doing. I ran into a yeoman who was stationed there who took me to his quarters and gave me a drink and told me where I could have some fun. He suggested that I try the Play Land at the beach type places where they have roller coasters and such stuff, so I did go there. While looking around I ran into a beautiful platinum blond about 19 years old who took a fancy to me and we went on all the rides and threw baseballs at bottles and all those carnival things. It was getting late and before we did much else I had to go to the john, while I was in there an old guy came up to me and told me to be on guard that there were a group of Aussies (reserve army) guys that looked as if they might be laying for me because I had this good looking girl, and they didn't. I thanked him and took this nice girl as fast as I could out of the park and grabbed a taxi and offered to take her home, which she accepted. I got her home safely and directed the taxi back to where the ship was tied up. I've never seen any taxi like this one before, it was running on a charcoal burner that stood on the running board on the drivers side. I was amazed that it could run at all. The taxi had to let me out at the gate about 100 yards away from the ships gang way. As I started walking towards the ship I saw a drunken marine lying on the ground near the gate, I knew he was from the ship so I asked the Aussie guard at the gate to help me boost him on to my shoulders so I could carry him back to the ship. I got him in the well known firemen's hold with a leg and arm together around my neck and proceeded to walk towards the ships gangway. When I got there at the bottom of the gangway the OD thought that I had decked the poor guy right there and I had to yell that I found him at the gate and had to carry him this far, so I carried him up to the quarter deck and then some marines took him off my hands and put him in his bunk. It bothered me to think that the O.D. thought I was fighting with this marine. Can you believe that after the war around 1947 I stopped for gas at a station in Portland, Oregon and here was that marine pumping gas and he recognized me! We had a big laugh remembering that episode. We left Melbourne and headed for Perth through the Tasmanian Straits. Our radio shack was located one deck below the bridge on the starboard side of our deck the Captain always held his Captain's mast penalty ceremony there. We had a port hole that look right out in that area, so while we were plowing on to Perth they had a captains mast going on. Much to my surprise a good friend of mine a marine corporal was being reprimanded for some violation and I watched as they stripped his corporal chevrons off and made him a first class private. Later on I asked him what he had done, his answer was that he hadn't done a watch the right way or something vague like that. We got to Perth and I had the duty so I stayed on board like a good sailor and watched everyone else go ashore. That afternoon some crazy Aussie pilot flew an A25 bomber right over the ship so close I could see the pilots face in the window. Late that night the O.D. called the radio shack and asked me to come down and help the communication officer to his quarters. I came down to the quarter deck and here is the very straight laced JG drunk as can be and not very coordinated. So with the help of the deck watch I got him down into the officer's quarters and left him. I sure razzed him on that one. The next thing I saw was the chief radioman dragging a bicycle up the gangway and leaving it on the quarter deck. Pretty soon along came a poor Aussie policeman looking for his bike. He came on board and claimed his bicycle but didn't press any charges. I was beginning to think that there must be a full moon out or something the way all these guys were acting.

Chapter 48.

The Indian Ocean & The Hoogily River!

We left Perth the next day and headed for Calcutta. We cleared the harbor and I was told that we would be picking up an escort the next day and we would be working him on the air with our TBY ultra hi-freq. Transceiver. I forgot to mention that the communication officer, the JG had been complaining that my operators were not copying the messages right because he couldn't break any of our messages. I told him that if the first two groups and the last to groups of the messages were exactly alike then the rest of the message had to be right or else he was setting up the decoder wrong. Right away he wanted to know if I knew anything about decoding machines and I denied that I even knew what they were. I figured if he ever knew that I decoded all the messages on that subchaser he would have had me doing the same thing for him. That was a close one and I breathed a sigh of relief.

While we were looking for our escort I happened to look out of the port hole and saw another court marshal going on. Guess what? It was my old marine buddy getting busted again, this time down to Private. I caught him again that night and asked what happened this time? He told me it was another dumb infraction. I told him he better not get anymore deck courts because he might be busted down to officer's steward second class or something awful.

We picked up our escort on the third day and made contact through the TBY xmter by phone. This was such a high frequency that we could use it because it transmitted only line of sight so we weren't worried about some one picking up our location or what kind of a ship we were. We used calls like White Horse and Charlie, this seemed to work out OK. The only problem we had with this ship was that it could hardly keep up with us, we actually slowed down several knots so as not to embarrass them. They escorted us for about three days then left us again on own. In the meantime we had plenty of general quarter drills and even had the passengers taking part in the drills in case of a sinking. We also had a drill where we put mine sweeping cutters out on cables just to see how they handled. These were put out on each side of the ship and they flared out about 200 feet away. It looked very awkward to handle and looked like trouble as far as I could see.

We were near the northern tip of Sumatra Island but not in sight of it when the midnight bridge crew spotted a silver streak coming towards the ship! They all stood on the wing except the helmsman and speculated as to what it was. It passed the ship about 50 yards in front of the bow and kept going, that's when they realized it was a torpedo. Now this was late in the war, so my theory was that a Japanese submarine tried a long shot at the ship and didn't want to waste more than one torpedo on us and miscalculated our speed. Lucky for us, it couldn't have kept up or tracked us as we were going too fast for any submarine at that time to be able to stay with us so it probably fired one shot hoping to hit us. I got to thinking what if it had hit us and we had to abandon ship out in the middle of the India Ocean with 500 Red Cross women on the ship as well as 5000 soldiers what a horrible disaster that would have been.

As we approached the Bay of Bengal I picked up a very poor CW signal calling our ship on 500 Kilo Hertz. This is the first time I ever heard any station call a ship by its true international call letters so I told the operator on that freq not to answer that call (This would let the enemy know we were in the area) and complained to the Lt JG and the Warrant Officer about this idiot calling us and identifying us on 500 where the signal travels quite a long ways like a 1000 miles or better depending on the time of day. In fact, it could travel half way around the earth during the night cycle. We never answered that signal and never found out who was sending that transmission which sounded as if he was sending it with his foot!

We finally entered the Hoogily River and we were on our way to Calcutta, which was approximately 75 miles up river. Upon entering the main channel of the river, I took the liberty of leaving the radio shack in order to view the country side. I could see both sides of the river and it was as if I was in fairy land. I could see a palace with its domes peeking above the lush tropical trees and the colors were spectacular. The terrain looked just like the jungle that I studied in my geography book in grammar school. I just couldn't believe that I was this lucky to see the real Indian Jungle. It all looked so mysterious to me and I felt as thrilled as could be. Even the vultures flying around above the trees looked like something out of a story book picture in a fairy tale story. Looking on the other side of the river I spotted another palace peeking above the trees. There must have been many other building that I couldn't see that were on the ground hidden amongst the huge growth of the jungle.

As we progressed up the river we passed small sail boats hauling supplies like barrels of oil or what ever and sacks of grain. Some of them had the load stacked high above what we would call the safety factor. These ships had the shape of a cocoa nut cut in half and they looked as if they displaced at about 20 tons. The helms man steered the ship with a huge sweep oar hanging off the middle of the stern; it was very picturesque. About this time the P.A. system was blaring out an announcement telling all hands and passengers please to stay exactly as they were as they have to balance the ship perfectly to pass through the next half of a mile of river as it is very shallow and they will only clear the bottom of the river by a half of a foot. The request was repeated again and emphasized how important it was to stay put, so I stayed out on deck an enjoyed the view as we slowly traveled over the shallow part of the river. Then came the announcement that all was clear and we could move about again. Later on I learned that the engineers had leveled the ship by shifting fluid around in the holding tanks for the right kind of balance. Back in the radio shack everything was going along fine and we got a message from the Calcutta Port Captain that the pilot would soon board us and take us to our anchorage. The Hoogily River was very wide where we anchored and we were told to put guards on the bow to keep saboteurs from getting near the ship with a possible bomb or a device to cause damage. We had our marine squad maintain vigilance by standing on the bow of the ship right at the flag staff and marching around it with a rifle on his shoulder. We kept this up for the whole time we were in this anchorage. We could see the docks where we would be taken to if we went ashore on liberty. While viewing the city I could see many of those minaret towers all over the city of Calcutta.

Another thing I noticed was many of those ugly looking vultures flying about. As I was taking all this in a C47 army transport flew by with the cargo door open and I could see an Air Force soldier standing by the door looking outside at the city and the river. Just as the plane started a turn by banking it flew into a group of those vultures and hit one of them as you could see the feathers floating down to the ground. I was told that the reason you see so many vultures flying around those minaret towers is that they have bodies placed up in the towers for some kind of religious ceremony, I don't know if someone is pulling my leg on that one or not.

On pay day we were paid in rupees and I don't know whether I got my right pay, for all I knew the paymaster could be making something on the exchange. While the troops and Red Cross Workers were being unloaded, the crew was given a lecture on how to act and respect the local religious groups and not to act like the ugly American. Our watch was given liberty this day and I decided to go ashore with my friend Max Hensely the marine that acquired all the deck court marshals. We hailed a rickshaw and told the ricksha driver to take us to the biggest hotel in town. He dropped us off in front of the Great Eastern Hotel, which did look like the best thing in town. So in we went and found that they were having a dance on the upper floor. We climbed up the wide stair case and saw that there was a very formal dance being held. We could see that most of the Red Cross girls we had on the ship were there along with some of our ships officers. I even caught sight of the Captain dancing with one of the good looking gals. After a couple of drinks we started to get feeling pretty good on what they called Lemon Squash which had a jigger of gin. The orchestra was an all Hindu band and they were playing the old time songs of the thirties. I noticed that Max was getting a little drunk on our gin and squash drinks and hoped that he wouldn't get to wild. All of a sudden he said to me, "I want the band to play the Marine Hymn." He got up, went up to the little band leader and said, "Play the Marine Hymn." The poor band leader didn't quite know what the Marine Hymn was. So he started somthing and it didn't sound like the Marine Hymn and Max got very angry and grabbed the poor old band leader by the neck tie and held him up off his feet and growled, "Played the god damn Marine Hymn now!" I jumped up from our table and ran towards the band stand yelling, "Max we have got to get the hell out of here before anyone recognizes us." I grabbed him by the arm and said, "Let go of this guy we've got to move". With that we both took off for the stair case and stumbled down the steps as fast as we could. Looking around for a place to hide I saw that the stair case had nothing under-neath it so I said to Max, "Lets get under the stairs as no one was paying any attention to us." Just as we dove underneath the stairs I saw the MP's and SP running up the stairs to the ball room. After they disappeared we casually got out from underneath the stair case and slowly walked out of the beautiful Great Eastern Hotel with its tropical overhead fans twirling away and I was thinking, "I'll never be able to come back to this place again." We got as far away as we could from the Hotel and found a funny little bar where we could get a drink. Max demanded a gin and tonic and what we got after much haggling due to a misunderstanding between English and Hindu, was another lemon squash and gin. We decided to leave with our drinks and Max walked right through the screen door without opening it. Of course the screen burst out of the frame and no one said anything to us so we kept going. I guess they were glad that we left without tearing the place apart. We hailed a rickshaw and told the driver to take us to the docks down by the river. Max yelled to the driver "Go as fast as you can," but the driver didn't change his speed so Max pulled off his belt and was going to belt him one in the back when I stopped Max and reminded him about the ugly American talk, so he put the belt back on which I was glad of because by this time as we were nearing the docks the sweat was running down this drivers back like a river. As we drew near the docks we could see our liberty boat at the docks loading up with crew members going back to the ship. On the talk of how you should handle your self while in India the word was not to over pay anyone for services, as it would only make things harder for the next group who have to do duty here. When the driver stopped and held out his hand saying 3 rupes we tossed him 1 rupee and took off for the liberty boat. There were about five or six rickshaw drivers standing there on the dock and when our driver started yelling that we hadn't paid him enough they all started chasing us down the dock. I thought I saw some knives being waved so I yelled at Max lets go and we ran at top speed and dove into the liberty boat just as it was pulling away from the dock leaving the mad rickshaw drivers shaking their fists at us as we headed for the ship. When we arrived at the gangway of the ship the OD sent down 2 seaman to help us up the ladder as he had watched the whole episode through his glasses and figured that we were too drunk to make it up the ladder. This was not the case as we assured the two seaman we were OK and that we could make it up to the quarter deck on our own power. When I got to the quarter deck and finished saluting the flag on the stern and I explained to the OD that the rickshaw driver was charging us to much money so we threw a rupee at him and ran like hell for the boat. Since it was already moving away from the dock we had to leap into it head first or we would have had to fight it out with a bunch of rag heads. He laughed and we went to our quarters. That night I was told that I would have to do shore patrol the next day starting at 0800.

The next morning I got up bright and early. It looked like a pretty good day, nice and sunny. I got dressed put on the canvas puttees, got the SP arm band and got ready for shore patrol. They drove me over to the Army Military compound and introduced me to my fellow MP, the man I was to work with. He looked pretty grouchy to me, no smile or salutations except a curt hello. This looked like a disagreeable day to me. We were told to walk around the city and only check out our Military personnel. We started walking slowly towards the center of the city. I began to see that we weren't going to have much trouble as there weren't that many military people running around. After checking out the hotels and night clubs like Firpo's and the Great Eastern Hotel my partner remarked that it was getting very warm and he knew a good place to cool off for awhile. He led me to a large downtown theater that said on the marquee, "Air Conditioned Theater." This was where we were going to hide for a little while. So in we went, without paying of course, and sat down and watched the movie in the loge seat area. I don't remember the movie but it was a British production any way and was very boring, I think I fell asleep. My partner shook me out of my dream world and said, "Come on we might as well get some lunch now." So off we trot to a British Military confine where they happily served us a scrumptious lunch. We took a turn through the ghetto block of buildings where there were many prostitutes carrying on their trade. They worked behind sack covered doorways with a single bunk in small rooms. It made me very nervous even to walk through the place as all I could think of was horrible diseases. I was very glad when we left the area. We went through the New Hog Market which was large barn like structure with lots of stalls with many different items for sale such as vegetables, fruit, clothes, shoes, jewelry, pottery and many other things. I even watch a Hindu fakir play a wind instrument and have a cobra snake come out of a basket swaying around as if it were hypnotized by the music. I didn't test the snake to see if it was under the flute players control · but it was just like you see it in the old movies about India. I finally finished the day and gladly went back to the ship in time for dinner. The next day I went down town just to look around. As I was walking around, two young kids were playing flutes and trying to beg for money, by chanting the Hindu word (boxie), they got irritated because I didn't offer them any money and made faces at me then ran away. Just then a very dignified Hindu man in a complete white robe that seemed to be flowing around him made a remark to me like "Little Rogues aren't they"! I laughed and agreed because it described them so beautifully. The street cars were always completely jammed with passengers of all descriptions, some with turbans, some with the white robes, some with suits and some with special uniforms and all with special colors which denoted their status in Indian society. On one corner I watched an untouchable give himself a washing while wearing his grey sheet and managing to do it with out disrobing. He was using the water that came out of a opening in the middle of the street, it came bubbling up about a 2 inches above the level of the street, I was told that this was the way it was all over the city. It probably was water from the Hoogily river. The final act in his cleaning was a scrubbing of his teeth with his fore finger, then he gave me a big smile, it was then that I noticed that his teeth and gums were as red as they could be. Asking around about the red teeth I found out that they were all chewing Betel nut, a mild drug inducing nut, ugh! Another thing that was fascinating but horrible was the fact that the City Government had to go around every morning to pick up all the people who had died during the night. These were the homeless and were mostly the untouchables. Walking down the street in the early morning you could see these people sleeping in doorways and along the side walks against the buildings.

The taxis in this town were mostly old touring cars made in the USA I think because they sure looked like some old models that I used to see when I was a child in the 1920's. Some were Flint's, Studebaker's and Nash's. Then there were the rickshaw's and they were two wheeled vehicles with two poles out front to be pulled by hand by drivers who looked as if they never had a full meal. They were scrawny looking but seemed to have plenty of energy. Then there were many wagons with two large wheels, being pulled by horses. The street cars looked ok but I never tried one because they were always full of natives hanging out of every conceivable place, like a crowd jumping on a local street car in San Francisco after a football game at Kezar Stadium.

On liberty there were several Red Cross tours for service men. I took advantage of two of them. One was a visit to the Jane temple and the other was to the Burning Ghats. We did both on the same day. At the Jane temple as we walked down the sidewalk we noticed that there were fish ponds on both sides. These ponds were covered with wire mesh so that birds could not get at the fish. The priests all had long handled fans and they swept the side walk in front of them so that they wouldn't step on any ants. Their belief was in reincarnation so they don't believe in causing the death of any animal or insect, as they could be one of those ants or fish or what ever. The temple was decorated with lots of colored glass and mirror like tiles all in little squares about half the size of a dime. After touring the temple with our shoes off we climbed on our tour bus and headed for the Burning Ghats down by the Hoogily River. On the way we stopped to do a little shopping. I managed to buy four thin silver bracelets which I put into my jumper pocket. We arrived at the Burning Ghats and were allowed to wander around the funeral fires so that we were able to see the beginnings of a body about to be cremated to the final stage where there were only the ashes. We were told that sandalwood was the most favored wood for the pyre depending on your wealth and status in life. The tour guide also told us of a custom where they take the belly button from the body and bury or push it into the mud on the banks of the Hoogily River which is part of the Ganges River, I believe, as the river runs past the Burning Ghats site. Just as she finished lecturing, a group of mourners came in with a body all decked out in flowers and was placed in a hollow bit of ground then they piled Sandal Wood over the body. There was lots of wailing and crying, with me right in the middle of all the relatives. The ships photographer took my picture standing there. He promised me a picture but I never ever got it. You remember me telling about putting those silver bracelets in my jumper pocket? When we got back to the ship I started to take off my white jumper and discovered that those silver bracelets were gone. Evidently some pretty good pickpocketers spotted them in my pocket and took advantage of my ignorance and picked up a nice set of bracelets for his girl friend or mother, or maybe just for some money.

Mean while back on the ship things were being unloaded and crew members were busy trying to get at some of the C rations that were being unloaded for the Army personnel. My Warrant officer came around the radio shack and complained to me that he thought he was getting Cholera, I asked him how he knew, his answer was that he had been going to the bathroom so much that he just knew that was what it was. I told him that he probably ate something that caused him to have the GI'S. That settle him down for the moment. While loading up with returning troops for the good ole USA, one of the GI's fell into one of our holds and broke his back, I sure felt sorry for him. We had tried warning all passengers of the hazards on the ship but I guess we missed that one.

One day the captain was showing visitors around the ship. I was going forward to talk to the marine on duty at the bow. As I passed the chain locker some one called out to me that they had some thing good to drink and would I like a shot. Here were two sailors pouring out some awful looking juice out of a water casket into a white under shirt, using it as a strainer, then squeezing it into a bucket. This juice had the same color as the Hoogily, they offered me a drink which I knew I shouldn't have but I did try it and it tasted awful. I left them and went back towards my quarters when all of a sudden I began to feel sick. I hurried to the head (bath room) and got there just in time to heave all that terrible stuff up. It came out like a fire hydrant turned on full force. I did mention that this drink had the color of the Hoogily river, a dirty yellowish brown. That cured me of trying any of that fruit and whatever mix again. I had gotten rid of it just in time because I felt better right away. So up to the bridge I went and was just going to enter the radio shack when I noticed that Max the marine was marching around the jack staff with the rifle on his shoulders just like he was marching on the parade grounds. Seeing him doing that I realized that he was sampling the drinks from the chain locker. Then I noticed that the skipper was on the bridge with all those visitor and they were all looking at Max doing his bit around the flag staff. Luckily they didn't look too long and they never caught on to the fact that Max was drunk. It's a wonder he didn't fall in the drink.

Chapter 49.

Different Route to USA!

By now we were loaded with Army Personnel from the Burma China campaign and a few Indian girls who had married G.I's, also there were a few Red Cross women. We were getting ready to start out for the trip down the river. We had a British pilot on board to guide us from the anchorage to the mouth of the river. After hoisting the anchor up I could see us starting to drift and the ship was gliding into the river bank as the pilot was trying to swing the bow around the wind kept it from swinging, so apparently he rang for slow ahead and the propellor evidently was already into the mud of the river bank because instead of going ahead the ship began to tilt on its side at about a fifteen degree angle, the bridge rang for stop and you could hear the turbines groan as the ship rolled back to level driving the turbine backwards. This must have been hard on all the gears including the prop as the skipper became very angry and told the pilot to leave the ship because he was going to handle it by himself. We drifted out into the middle of the channel and the skipper started us down the river at a pretty good clip. Standing on the stern I could see we were going pretty fast. We were throwing a bow wave of about ten feet and you could see it washing over the banks on the rivers edge. At one point I saw some folks get washed back down the banks as the wave crested the top, I wondered about this Ugly American stuff. Some one said we were going to try and get past that

21 foot depth hazard before a certain time because that was when the tide began to recede and if we didn't make it on time we would be delayed for another day. Just then I looked ahead of the ship as we were rounding a bend in the river and saw a small harbor where there were five or six of those native sailing vessels anchored. I could see a seaman rapidly pulling up his anchor and looking at us with disbelief. I could see that he had even gotten to the point where he could have started pulling the anchor out of the mud when the ten foot wave hit him it lifted the boat high out of the water bow first and then the stern rose up afterwards, the action of the bow lifting up so fast flipped him in the air about 20 feet and into the water he went, not only that all 5 or 6 ships sank quickly to the bottom of the harbor as they were swamped by the wave action. My first thought was that poor guy just lost his ship and he probably will never get

compensated. On the other hand we did sink 5 or 6 ships during this war! Wow, I think the skipper must have been pretty mad because at one time I thought I saw several children swept off the banks on the other side of the dikes. Well we made it over the shallow spot and everyone had to stay where they were again till we made it past this obstacle. We hit the Bay of Bengal and started out towards the west, meaning that we were going towards the Suez Canal. On the way we stopped at Colombo Harbor, in Ceylon. Knowing that Ceylon was one of the largest suppliers of tea, I was wishing that I could purchase a large quantity for my folks but I knew that would be to hard to accomplish since I didn't have liberty. Why we stopped there wasn't explained and no one was to interested as everyone wanted to get back to the states. Ceylon was renamed Sri Lanka after the war. We upped anchor and progressed on towards Aden the entrance to the

George C. Larsen

Red Sea. As we were traveling along at a very good clip in the Red Sea we could see the Sahara Desert kicking up a large cloud of sand from the winds that blow across her desert. Late in the afternoon the sky turned red from this desert sand; now I could see how this sea got its name. Every once in awhile we would sight one of those funny little native sail boats that plied the area carrying supplies to all those small sea ports, or they might have been fishing for a living. One day a water tender from the engine room told me that the water temperature from the sea that they were taking on was 92 degrees Fahrenheit! No wonder we noticed the heat. All I could think of was a nice ice cold Coco Cola. They did serve a cool drink similar to a Coke but nothing as good as I remembered them. One of the quartermaster took a fresh egg and cracked it open and laid it on the deck where it fried to a crisp just as if it was in a hot frying pan. Everyone was having trouble sleeping with this infernal tropical heat. It seems that we had been in hot weather ever since we left San Pedro, California. We entered the Suez Canal which looked just like a big ditch. You could see bomb and shell damage and there were work crews repairing the damage all along the canal. Of course we had to pay for going through the Canal and we were charged by the number of passengers we had on board. The Captain allowed Egyptian vendors on board the ship to sell leather goods like purses, belts and cigarettes cases. I chased them away from the radio shack as I didn't think they should even be on this deck.

We got to Port Said and I took a liberty just to see what it was like. While wandering around town I had a slightly built teenager trying to get me to watch him perform a trick with my money. So I gave him a ten piasters Egyptian paper bill. He did some fancy hand movements and handed me back a one piasters bill. Being the tight wad I stepped on his foot, which kept him from escaping, and demanded my ten piasters bill back. At first he stalled but when I reached into my jumper as if to pull out a knife or gun he quickly gave me my money back and I gave him his one piasters. A crowd of Egyptian natives began to crowd around us and I explained in a loud voice that this kid was trying to con me. There was a liquor store in this small square so I ducked into it and looked around just to get away from the crowd that had gather out side. Thinking that I should buy something I bought half pint of Egyptian malt whiskey. I left the shop and walked around the town until I spotted a military beer garden for the Allies. I went and sat down at a table where a British merchant mariner was sitting. We introduced ourselves and started talking about the war. We both ordered a draft beer and had a great time relating our experiences. The beer tasted as if it had flowed through a bunch of straw, at least it smelled like straw water but was better than nothing. I left for the ship soon after and before going aboard I stuffed the half pint of booze into one of my boots where if seemed to fit perfectly so that I could smuggle it aboard. The OD never detected it so I made it to my locker and stowed the half pint for some future use.

Before we left Port Said I had the luck to actually see a bunch of native stevedores loading coal on an old coal burning tramp steamer. What was unique about this loading work was the way it was being done. There were two long gangways going up to the holds of this tramp steamer and the stevedores were carrying sacks of coal on their backs up the one gangway and then walking down the other gangway for another load. This looked like what could have been a bunch of slaves at work in another century. I watched this procedure for about 15 minutes, it was so unusual. I also saw familiar signs on the fuel storage tanks that dotted the shore line, like Shell, etc.

We finally left Port Said behind and started out in the Mediterranean sea, going past such famous places that had been bombed just a few weeks ago in the war like Malta, Sicily and Italy. When we passed the Rock and entered the Atlantic ocean a soldier standing on the stern complained to me that we were going too slowly. I pointed to a ship just on the horizon ahead of us and said to him, "See that ship, I want you to tell me were it is when I come back in about 45 minutes," as I recognized it as a liberty ship doing about 10 knots. I came back in about 45 minutes and he had to admit that we must be going quite a bit faster as we had passed that ship and it was astern of us now.

When I relieved the watch for our first night on the Atlantic I was told by the watch standers that they had reported an incident that had happened on their watch. It seems that the executive officer was entertaining some Red Cross ladies out behind the radio shack and they were drinking beer. The Exec. began throwing the empty bottles against the radio shack wall and the supervisor on watch reported this to the bridge. Nothing was done about it and I began to worry about what the exec would do to our group because I knew he didn't like us. Nothing came of it but I told my group to watch out for the Exec.

So far the trip was uneventful but about the time we got to the middle of the Atlantic we hit a pretty good storm. The stern lifted out so high that the 27 foot screw was completely in the air for a second. When I went up to the radio shack I had to be careful because the split in the deck out side of our radio shack came completely apart each time the bow came up out of the water. All the guys on my watch were seasick especially when I came in eating a spam sandwich. They filled up both wastebaskets. Things settled down again and we enter the Chesapeake Bay and headed for the Norfolk Navy Yard.

Chapter 50.

Surprises In Norfolk.

Once in the yard we settled down to routine clean up and necessary repairs. The first night at sunset when we struck our colors the bugler did a little fancy rendition of our ceremony by swinging the call. The very next morning we got a very nasty note from the admiral in charge of the yard on our poor style of doing colors. That very first day, I forgot to mention, the only personnel that left the ship was the Executive Officer and those who were with him on that fateful night where they were

427

slamming beer bottles against the radio shack. The rumor was that the Captain kicked them off the ship never to return according to the skippers Chief Yeoman.

The next morning I found out I had liberty for that day, so off I went to see what the city of Norfolk looked like. Before I left the ship I remembered that my friend Kirby Jones the gunners mate from the cruiser St. Louis was from this city and that his father was the Fire Chief for the Norfolk fire department and his brother worked in one of the down town fire houses. So, I headed for the nearest fire house to inquire as to where Kirby Jones house might be. The first firehouse I came to wasn't too far away from the Norfolk Navy yard, so I stopped in and asked if any one there know where the Kirby Jones house was. Much to my surprise one fireman said, "Sure I know where it is, in fact his brother is stationed at this house". He gave me directions to their house which was only about two blocks away. It must have been about 2:30 PM in the afternoon when I knocked on the door and a nice looking mother type lady opened the door and said, "Hello could I help you?" I said yes, "I'm a friend of Kirby's, my name is George Larsen, she gasp and said, "come in quickly I want you to talk on the phone!" Not knowing what was up I got on the phone and said, "Hello," the voice said, "Hello Kirby how did you get home so fast?" Right then I recognized the voice as my very own mother's voice and I said, "No this isn't Kirby this is your son George!" She said, "What?" I repeated what I had said and she said, "How in the world did you get there?" Remember I had left home saying that I would be back in a couple of weeks after our shake down cruise. After she got things straightened out as to who was there she told me that she was calling Mrs. Jones to tell her that Kirby was on his way home by train on leave and should be there in three or four days. What a small world this is. I had a nice conversation with my mother and a nice visit with the Joneses. They said to be sure and come back when Kirby got home and I said that I would. The next day I had the duty and was sitting in the radio shack with my crew on watch in the late afternoon when I had a phone call from the OD on the quarter deck that I had a visitor coming up to the radio room to visit me, his name was Lt. jg. Berryman. How he always found me I'll never know, anyway I thought maybe I can impress these guys when he steps through the door. Scott came in through the door and one of the watch standers yelled "Attention". I looked up and said out loud, "why you old son of a bitch, how the hell are you?" Well, you should have seen the looks on all four guys in that room. I think that they could see me being led to the brig right now, except Scott broke out with a big grin and said, "How the hell are you Swede?" "Come on your going on liberty with me." I said, "I can't, I've got the duty," he replied, "No I got you off, go get dressed an we can whoop it up tonight." After introducing him to every one I went down and got into my liberty clothes and we took off for Newport News, which is across the bay from Norfolk. We had a blast and decided to get a hotel room because the ferry had quit running for the night. Naturally I got sick from to much alcohol. The next morning we caught an early ferry and I made it back to the ship with a big hang over and Scott told me to come over to his ship that next night and he would show me around his" tub." He told me he was the navigator on his ship the Gen. Randal a two stack transport larger than our ship.

When I started over it began to rain and the wind was blowing rather hard, I was told that it was the tail end of a hurricane, which I believed. Having never been in one I was glad we were in port. Berryman met me on the quarter deck and showed me all through the bridge and chart room and the radio shack and we had a nice visit. We parted at the gangway and I didn't' see him again until after the war.

A couple of days later I got a message that my sister Dagmar, who had enlisted in the Coast Guard in 1944, was coming up from Charleston to visit me. I went over to the Jones house hold and asked Mrs. Jones if Dag could stay at their house when she got to Norfolk. In the meantime Kirby arrived home, so we planned some night time parties for the three of us when Dagmar arrived. Some how she got a ride in a Navy Plane or Army Plane I never did find out but she arrived and we all got together and went to Virginia Beach where they had a dance and we all had a good time. It sure seemed funny, here we are on the East Coast doing about the same things that we did out on the West Coast. In the meantime I found out that we were going to leave port soon, so I asked my sister to be on her way back to Charleston, as I didn't think it was very wise to stay in Norfolk by her self. So she dutifully went back to the Coast Guard barracks in Charleston and I went back to my ship to get ready for another trip.

To my surprise we sailed out of Chesapeake Bay with no troops or passengers. We still didn't know where we were going. The Atlantic Ocean seemed very calm and we could see that we were heading east towards Europe. On the way some one in the crew managed to steal five gallons of strawberry ice cream from the freezer by breaking the lock. This brought on a big search for culprit. This brought on great laughter amongst the crew as they watched the head of that department search for clues. This episode seemed to relax the crew as we all knew that the ice cream was going to the officers mess anyway. Around the fifth day we saw the cliffs of Dover or thought we did. We were in the English Channel and steaming along at a brisk pace. One of my operators copied an urgent message warning all ships at sea to be on the watch out for mines in the English Channel that had broken loose during the last storm. I rushed this message up to the bridge and heard the comment, "Is that what those buoys are that are bouncing around in the waves!". I thought, "Oh brother I hope we don't run into a mine now after all the miles we have gone so far." Luckily we made it to our destination just out side of La Harve, where we picked up a French pilot to guide us into the harbor. We heard the skipper invite the pilot to breakfast and he laughed then he said, "No but I wouldn't mind having lunch with you." Then he explained that they not only had daylight saving time but that they also had a new one called war saving time which meant that we were off of local time by two whole hours. As we slowly moved into the harbor I had a chance to observe the whole city from the piers to the hills in back of the city. The city was completely leveled, the former submarines pens on the waters edge were smashed to bits from heavy shelling and bombs. The cathedral near the center of town had only one corner of the building still standing and it looked like a sharp pointed dagger made of shredded bricks & plaster. It stood about three stories high and looked awesome. We tied up at a temporary dock and settled in for whatever the Army Command wanted us to do. We saw many German prisoners working on the docks with a whole bunch of Army Guards standing around armed to the teeth and looking very mean. A couple of the crew members thought it would be cute to try out their German on the prisoners but they were chased away by the guards who yelled at them for even getting near those guys. They gave them holy hell and cursed them to blue heaven. I thought good for them, those guys had just finished a tough fight and weren't about to let those prisoners have any comfort at all. Around 11 PM we noticed that it was still daylight, this was astounding to us having lived further south than this we had never experienced this phenomenon. Of course that two hour time saver helped. We got permission to play soft ball on the docks at midnight and had a lot of fun just because of the unusual day light at night. The next day I took a liberty and ventured into town. I happened to have several bars of expensive soap in my locker, so I thought maybe I could barter or trade for something while roaming around the city. While walking towards the city I noticed the that the public rest rooms were just open air compartments, no roofs and stood about five feet high so that you could see a person from their shoulders up while standing in the there. As I was walking on the other side of the street I noticed a well dressed French man with a straw hat on; going to the bathroom. As he was doing his stuff a women walked by and as she passed by him while he was doing his thing he tipped his hat to her and gave her a big smile! I almost fell into the sidewalk laughing so hard on seeing this little act. Both genders use the same bathroom so I guess it wasn't unusual for something like that to happen here in France. I had come ashore with that bar of good smelling soap which happened to be Cashmere Bouquet, so I decided to take a ride on the only street car running. It had a sign that said it was going to Rhone so I hopped on and stood up near the end platform and took out my bar of soap. I held it in my hand and every one on the street car was staring at it. Then I started tossing it in the air and catching it. Every pair of eyes followed the bar up and down as I played with it.

Some of the passengers started to bid on it as if it were an auction. I soon got tired of tossing it and decided that I would give it away rather than trying to make a crummy couple of bucks with it. I noticed a little old man dressed rather poorly, so I motioned him to come over and I handed him the bar of soap. You should have seen his face light up when he realized that I was giving it to him for nothing. He put it up to his nose and took a deep breath smelling its perfume and then he happily put it in his pocket while thanking me profusely. I didn't want to go to Rhone so I jumped off at the next stop and walked back to the center of the city. Years later I found out that street car did not go to the city of Rhone but was going to Rhone Blvd.

Back in the main part of the torn up city I stopped at a tavern to try a shot of cognac. Much to my surprise I was handed a shot of cognac in a shot glass that had several big chips in the rim of the glass, then I noticed that everyone had a broken glass. I guess it was to early for any replacement glasses to be made. The fighting had been over for only about a month so you couldn't expect things to shape up instantly. The cognac didn't taste that great so I decided to go back to the ship.

When I got back I saw that they were loading up troops for the trip home. When we were loaded to the hilt we started out of the harbor and headed for the states. The trip across the Atlantic was uneventful with the exception of a lot of trading of souvenirs between soldiers, sailors and others. I was dickering with a soldier who had a German P38 pistol. I was trying to trade a Indian pearl handled dagger for the P38. I almost convinced him that my dagger was worth more than his gun. He decided not to trade the gun so I gave up. We entered New York Harbor in the early morning and it was a beautiful sight to sail past the Statue of Liberty. We docked at a pier on the Hudson River. A bunch of us old timers got off the ship and ran across the street to a bar for a quick drink. While in there we noticed a very drunken women mooching drinks off of any one she could. She came by us and we decided to stick her on to our chief warrant who was having drink down at the other end of the bar. We told her he always bought ladies a drink, so go down and give him a big kiss and he will come through with a drink. Poor William the warrant couldn't get rid of her as she was hanging all over him and he didn't know how to deal with her. We all left to go back to the ship with him trying to get untangled from her. Once out side we were all laughing so hard it was pitiful. Then we started for the pier but lo and behold the ship wasn't there it had vanished. Some one spotted it up the road apiece at pier 42 where the Normandie had caught on fire and sank under the heavy dosage of water the fire department had given it. It sank because it rolled over from the unbalance of water it was getting, I believe. While in port I was told to get all the Fox Sked messages that we missed while in the India Ocean. So I went down to the quarter deck to use the phone to get a ride to the Navy message and communication center downtown New York. When the transportation office answered my phone call I said "this is Lt. Comdr. Larsen, "Can you send a car and driver to pier 42 to the Gen Greely for transportation to the communication office?" They replied, "Of course sir right away." The OD was listening and laughed and shook his head in wonderment. I went back up to the radio shack to wait for my ride. It came in about 15 minutes as I got a call from the OD saying, "your car is here Larsen." When I got down to the quarter deck there was a sea man 1st/class waiting for his rider. He didn't pay much attention to me until I said, "I'm the guy you are going to take to the communication center." I explained that I knew I would get the car faster if I used the Lt Comdr designation rather than a radio man 1st class. I said, "Don't worry this will be an easy job for you." So off we go to the center. When I got to the center I found out that the elevator operators were on strike and the office I wanted to go to was on the 12th floor. I had to hike up all 12 flight of stairs to get there. A chief came up to me and asked, "What can I do for you?" and I said, "I would like Fox sked messages from 1234 to 2906 all the messages in between we could not copy. He growled something about what was the matter with us couldn't we copy the Fox Sked. I retorted, "No but we could have if they could get a signal out into the Indian Ocean were we spent quite a few days. In fact we could only get British signals from Melbourne to Gibralter." He didn't have anything to say and went back into some room a came up with all the numbers. I thanked him and went back down to the car and went back to the ship thanking the driver for the ride.

The next day I went on liberty thinking that a nice steak would be great for lunch. So I stopped in a fancy bar around Times Square and ordered a filet mignon. The waiter asked me if I was sure I wanted a filet mignon because they were pretty expensive, I said, "Yes that is what I want." While waiting for my meal I had bottle of beer. The steak came and it looked delicious and was, in fact it was the best I had ever had and was worth the money. I think it was around 15 dollars with the tip, which was quite a lot for the times.

Chapter 51.

Seven Days Leave.

We were going to be in New York for quite awhile so I put in for a weeks leave with the idea of going to Charleston to visit my sister Dagmar. I sent her a telegram that I was coming down and went into Eastern Airline ticket office and obtained tickets for Charleston. I left the ship and made a reservation at a small hotel down town and spent the early evening carousing around Times Square looking at all the sights. I put in a wake up call for six o'clock the next morning. I took a taxi to

Laguardia Airport and found the Eastern Airline terminal was a little shed like building where the passengers waited for their ride. Soon we boarded the DC3 and took off. When we were at our flying elevation we began to hit some rough weather. The plane was bouncing around a bit when all of a sudden there was a very loud boom and crackling. I saw lightning flash by the ship and we dropped about 20 feet at the same time. Everyone looked nervous and I wondered whether they had parachutes on these planes, as this was my first commercial flight. I reached under the seat and found something like a tubular shaped bag with a lid on it which I held up into the light to look at not knowing what it was at first. Then it dawned on me that it was a bag to throw up in. Well guess what, several passengers had seen me put this bag up in the air and they immediately began to throw up into similar bags, I guess that the suggested motion I

445

made pushed them over the edge as we were still jumping around in this rough weather. We finally arrived in Washington DC and landed at the airport after circling the Washington Monument which was a spectacular scene. I was told if I wanted to get off and stretch my legs to please put a magazine on the seat to show that it was occupied by a passenger who would be coming back on board. I walked around the terminal and thought to myself, at least I can say I was in Washington DC. We took off again and flew over lots of green forest and landed again at Winston-Salem where the plane heated up quickly from the burning sun. I got off the plane and grabbed a Coca Cola out of a machine in an old shed near the plane. We took off again and the plane cooled off a bit. Then we landed at Raleigh where it got hot on the plane again, we took off again and landed at Charleston. It was really hot. I got a taxi and rode into town directly to the Coast Guard Spar barracks. A nice Spar, by the name of Gene Worely, met me at the front door and told me she was to entertain me at the barracks until my sister arrived from Savannah! She told me that my sister had been transferred to Savannah just a couple of days ago, and being a friend of hers she said, "I'm to stay with you until she arrive's some time today, as she didn't have time to tell you about her transfer." So the first thing she suggested was that we play a little Ping Pong in the recreation room. We played for a long time and late in the afternoon my sister arrived. We soon started out for Savannah on a Greyhound Bus. It was getting close to evening. This bus seemed to stop at every little town on the way. At one stop we picked up a black US Army Warrant Officer who sat down in the middle of the bus and the driver told him to go to the back of the bus. The officer started arguing with the driver and the driver wouldn't start the bus until the black officer sat in the back seat. They argued for about 5 minutes and finally the black officer gave up and went to the back of the bus. This was the first time that I noticed how different the South was from the rest of the country. I did see the two different rest rooms land drinking fountains in Norfolk but it didn't register with me as to how bad it really was. I thought that the black officer had a right to sit where ever he wanted to. After all he was fighting for the country the same as the rest of us.

The ride to Savannah took all night and we arrived at the bus stop down town at about 6 AM. Dag had to get back to the barracks that morning so I walked her to the bus terminal that went out to the Island where she was based. She said to meet her that afternoon and we could go out to dinner and have a pleasant get together. I told her I would be looking for a place to stay right away. While waiting for her bus transportation to the Spar barracks, I met some of Coast Guard guys that were stationed there. We exchanged names and ships identity, one person I remembered was a sailor named Clarke Dittmer because 'he was stationed on board the CGC "Aggie" W126, a sister ship to the Tiger Maru! After I put my sister on the bus for the trip to the barracks, I started out for a hotel which I found down town. It was a small one which I . figured I could afford, I entered it and found a lady behind the counter, so I asked her if she had a room and her reply was very weird. She said, "We have a room but no bah?" So I said, "Thank you, I'll look around." What I thought she had said, was that the room had no bed and I was wondering how one slept in a room like that?

So off I went looking for another hotel. In the mean time I discovered that I didn't have much money in my wallet, this disturbed me and I could not think of how I lost about 300 dollars between

New York and Savannah? I was panic stricken and thought I had better wire good old dad for about 350 dollars out of my bank account in Mill Valley, so I went to Western Union and sent him a telegram asking for the money. Since it was early in the morning yet, the telegram arrived in San Francisco in time to enable my dad to get to the bank and send the money that day. The Western Union operator said it would get in to the office around 5 P M if every thing went right. So I planned to come back around that time before I was going to meet my sister. In the mean time I still had no place to stay so I went back to that original hotel and asked if that room was still available, which it was. Much to my surprise, the room had a bed. Thinking over what the lady had said in her southern accent was that there was no bath room not no bed. Naturally the bath room was down the hall.

Since I left the ship without any toilet gear, I decided I had better get a shave at a barber shop. So off I went to get a hair cut and shave. I went back to the Western Union office after that as it was close to 5 o'clock to see if my money order was there. There was a different operator on and he said, "Yes that there was a money order for George C. Larsen and did I have any identification on me." I said yes, "My California drivers license," which I proceeded to pull out of my wallet, when lo and behold 300 hundred dollars came out with the drivers license. It seems as though I had hidden that money in my wallet because I was afraid some one would try and steal it from me when I was in New York. So there I was with over 600 hundred dollars instead of just a few bucks. After settling with Western Union I went back to where I was to meet Dagmar. Looking around the city I was impressed with all the statues of Army Officers riding horses and holding swords up in the air. The pigeons didn't have much respect for the statues as most of them had decorted the hats of these soldiers and some of their noses. I met Dag and some of her friends and we had a good time. She told me that she had to work the next few days and I decided I would go back to New York and finish out my weeks leave in the Big Apple. Getting a return flight to New York was fairly easy, since I was in uniform, so I made a flight for the next morning. We said good bye and left knowing that we wouldn't see each other till after the war! I went back to the hotel and planned to take a shower in the available bath or "bah" room. I mention this as I had never been in such high humidity before. It took me five minutes to peel off my white jumper as it stuck to my body like glue and I had to fight it off, pulling and dragging the jumper as it came over my head slowly. All the time I'm sweating and thinking, this isn't my kind of country, I'll take the Northern climate any day.

The next morning I boarded the Eastern Airline flight to New York. We landed at several southern cities on our way North. When we got to Philadelphia the stewardess informed us that the weather in New York was questionable so we would have to stay on the ground in Philly till they got an OK to fly on, saying that any one who wanted to could catch the electric train that ran between Philly and New York which would get them in into New York in about two hours. I chose to wait at the airport and take my chances on the plane ride. We took off in about two hours and arrived over New York shortly. The pilot announced that we were going to have to circle New York for a while as the airfield was fogged in. We flew around Coney Island amusement park about three time as I could see the roller coaster lights as they looped around the track. There were several GI'S on the plane besides myself and we all ran out of cigarettes at about the same time so we asked the stewardess to break out the sample cartons that we knew she had. She reluctantly gave us each a four cigarette package because of our complaining voices. (I think that they were reluctant because they probably used them for black market purposes on the ground.) Any way, we finally landed and I quickly found a hotel in the down town area. I was lucky because it was getting close to midnight and I didn't' want to have to go back to the ship sleep. The next morning I called the ship and told my buddies where I was staying and I invited them to come up and help me spend the rest of my leave carousing around Times Square, etc. We had a great time and I met some good looking girls from Connecticut at the Roger's Corner night club. We had a great time and we roamed the clubs together until closing time. They were going back to Connecticut in the morning and invited me to come to the station and bid them good bye, which I did. It was great fun.

My shipmates told me that the ship was going to have a ships dance at the Waldorf Astoria Hotel and that it was for the whole crew. It was going to start around seven o'clock in the evening so we started out by warming up in several bars before deciding to grab a taxi for the hotel. When it was time to get going we hailed a taxi out in front of the last bar we were in and all jumped into this taxi and told him we wanted to go to the Waldorf Astoria Hotel. The taxi driver looked back at us with a very perplexed expression on his face. He didn't start out right away but just sat there with this funny look and said, "Okay guys if you want a ride around the block just for the ride I can do it but the Waldorf Astoria entrance is right here about ten steps away from this cab." Boy did we look foolish. We all gave him a tip and piled out of his cab quickly we were so embarrassed. We found the rooms where our ships party was being held and arrived just a little after seven. Every one from the ship that didn't have the duty was there. It was a great party and every one had a good time. We had a fine dinner and the usual dessert cake and coffee. They had a good dance band, and every one was dancing but me. I hung out at the bar and had a good night drink and left the party to return to the ship.

Chapter 52.

Back to Calcutta!

My leave was up and the ship was getting ready to leave the harbor with a whole ship load of Army recruits. Just as we were leaving the harbor for the open sea we heard a news broadcast that a B 25 Bomber had crashed into the Empire State building, in the early morning, while flying in a thick fog that surrounded the building at the higher levels. We heard that it hit so hard that it even broke loose some of the elevators. They didn't say how may casualties there were but we all thought of

457

how horrible it must have been for the people in the building, beside those in the plane who probably never knew it happened.

On the way out we found that we were on our way to Calcutta again! The trip on the Atlantic was uneventful. While walking around the deck for exercise one morning I noticed that we were passing some islands which I figured were the Azores which is just off the coast of Portugal. While looking at them I over heard some soldier telling this group that we were going past the Hawaiian Islands, I thought to myself I wonder who his geography teacher was in grammar school. I didn't tell them about the mistake because I didn't want to embarrass the guy who was telling about the location. In the Mediterranean Sea we got a call from the South African Naval Station in the city of Cape Town, which is on the very southern tip of Africa. They had a 200 group message for us. We were just off of the city of Alexandria as we could see the lights from her streets, (that's how close we were). They said that they were given the message, which they got by land line from the radio station in Alexandria, to relay to us as they couldn't raise us in their area.

Since the Germans had surrendered we were allowed to communicate on the air in this area as the Japanese couldn't possibly be picking up any of our transmissions. The operator in Cape Town thought it was funny that they could get us but Alexandria couldn't. We thought it was a strange thing also.

We finally arrived in Port Said in the early evening and I got a chance to see the outer harbor before entering the area where we would be going through the Suez Canal. You could see how much damage the war had done by counting the masts from sunken merchant ships that sat on the bottom of this shallow bay. I started counting the masts that

I could see and got up to 160 separate masts sticking out of the water. It was a revalation to me as to the damage that was done in that bloody conflict in North Africa. I hadn't seen this damage before when we went through as I had the duty at the time and was kept quite busy. As we waited to enter the Canal our wonderful Chaplain decided it would be great to take some of the crew over to the Sphinx at Gaza on a bus tour and pick up the ship at the other end of the Canal. This was a great idea except he choose to take the whole ships band and no other persons. This didn't set too well with me as I thought of the guys like our marines who had fought in Guadalcanal and all of the sailors who had done extensive duty in the South Pacific that should have had an opportunity to go, not a bunch of band players who had never been any where but New York. This made me mad and I thought I would do something to get back at this Chaplain. The first thing I did, which I should have done a long time ago was to find out where this band was quartered. To my surprise I found out that they were quartered on the port side of the ship in nice compartments with a private bath and bunks for six person each, this was located right across from the chiefs quarters. The first thing I did was go to my communication officer, a Lt Jr grade whose name I have forgotten, and complained about these band members getting better facilities than some of the regular petty officers. I had to explain the ranking of petty officers and that band personnel were rated the lowest on the ranking system. He finally got the picture and went to the Captain to have our quarters changed. This put all the band except the Chief in the crews quarters up forward where the bunks were 4 high and every one from seaman 2nd class and up to petty officers 2nd class slept and lived on board ship. That afternoon I moved into the after quarters next to or across from the chiefs on the port side of the stern section of the ship. Along with myself I found that they had moved in a gunners mate first class, a pharmacist mate first class, a cook first class, who was call Jack of The Dust for what ever reason I don't know, a first class store keeper who was in charge of the ice storage and all of that function and a first class electricians mate. We all had separate bunks and a huge head (bath room) with a great shower and plenty of room. Boy we thought we were living high on the hog, which we were by any military standards. We wondered about that Chaplain but didn't hold any grudge against chaplains, it just didn't sit well with us when we finally figured out what we had been missing.

We passed along the canal slowly and I had a chance to view the wrecked wheel houses and junk that laid along the edges of the canal. They were probably pulled from it during the war after a bombing raid by either side. About half way along the canal I was watching the drop of the wall of water off of the stern, it looked as if it were about 4 feet in depth as we plowed along the canal with not much clearance on either side of the ship. We apparently were pushing a lot of water ahead of us and when it got to the stern you could see why we made that 4 foot drop. As we passed a work barge loaded with large heavy rocks, that were being used as rip-rap, the barge dropped suddenly because of the four foot drop at the stern when we passed it. The barge was tied to the bank with only two heavy hawsers one on each end, so when she made that sudden drop it snapped both lines and the barge slowly drifted out into the middle of the canal. Since she was unattended I wondered who and how they were going to get her back to the proper work place. I never ever found out as we were going to be out of its sight in about a half an hour. Before we left the canal we stopped to pick up the bus party and they were told of their new quarters. I don't know what that chaplain thought but he had another encounter with us while in the Red Sea. He came dashing into the radio shack and demanded the news that was coming in on a BBC news cast. I happened to be on watch and told him I couldn't give it to him as the captain got it first. I also told him that this was a restricted area that he was not allowed to be in there. So I threw him out verbally and he rushed up to the bridge to complain to the captain about the treatment we gave him. The captain told him that everything we said to him was right and to stay out of that area. This was the second time some one complained about being wronged by me. The first one was when a colonel in the Army complained about my bumping him off the ladder during a General Quarters Alarm exercise. He had gone up to the bridge and complained bitterly about being bumped off the ladder by me and the captain told him to get the hell off the bridge and stay out way of his crew (during any actions they might need). The crew had a lot of respect for Captain Steadman because he stuck up for us when we were right. We passed through the Red Sea and the Chaplain gave a talk to any one who wanted to listen all about the places where Moses took the Israelites across the Red Sea where it had parted to let them escape from the Egyptians. He gave a theory on the tides and so on that it may have been one of those extremely low tide conditions and they were just going across at the right time.

We passed Aden and broke out into the Indian ocean and were on our way. I was copying a new broadcast from a British CW station when I copied a very strange story about a US Air Force plane dropping one single bomb that had the enough explosive power to blow up a whole city and it had dropped one of these on the Japanese city of Hiroshima. The news said that it had the explosive power of about 425 railroad car loads of dynamite. This was quite a story which I quickly passed up to the bridge. Then we copied lots of messages on negotiations with the Japanese High Command on an un-conditional surrender. A few days later we copied another story where the Air Force had dropped another bomb, called a nuclear bomb, on Nagasaki and wiped out a great portion of the city. There were more stories on negotiations and soon the word was out that the Japanese Emperor had made a speech that they were going to surrender immediately, which they did much to the joy of every one on the ship. The news was printed up when it was official and passed out to all the troops and crew. After the announcement was made the Captain had the gun crews fire some five inch star shells in celebration of winning the biggest war ever! While walking around the ship on deck, soldiers kept asking me if we were going to turn around and go home. Being I nice guy I told them, "Hell no!" "You guys are going to relieve a bunch of poor GI'S that have been fighting in the Burmese jungles and elsewhere, while you guys were still only training in the safety of the good old USA." This didn't sit well with them but I let them know how I felt about the chances of turning around was for them. We entered the Hoogily River and did the same old routine at the shallow spot in the river and proceeded on up to Calcutta. When we got there we were put into a closed off basin, something like a dry dock or a locked type lake, off the river which meant we couldn't use our toilets or showers because we would pollute the little lake or bay we were in. This meant that they had to put portable pots out for us. They were a bunch of toilets screened off with burlap material and there must have been at least 25 of these compartment like things all in a row. What a sight! While hanging out on the stern of the ship I noticed a beggar in a little poorly constructed skiff yelling Boxie, Boxie at us which I knew was their word for give me something. So I went down to my locker and got out a bar of that yellow GI soap that is as strong as you can get and brought it top side to toss to this beggar figuring he would probably sell it to some laundress. So I tossed it down to him and he caught it nicely and gave a big smile then to my amazement he took a huge bite out of that bar and began to chew it like candy. I didn't stay to see if he had a reaction from eating that bar but I knew that it had plenty of harsh chemicals in it that surely would eat out his stomach. I hope he had a strong stomach or he spit what he had in his mouth out.

The next morning I found out that I had shore patrol duty again. When I reported for duty I had the same MP that I worked with the last time. I smiled and greeted him like a friend and he gave me the cold shoulder as if he had never seen me before, so I reciprocated by not saying another word to him during the whole patrol. (I don't know what gives with guys like that but they must think that they are above acknowledging a friendly greeting.)

We ended up our patrol in Firpo's Bar and Restaurant where it seemed that half the CBI Army (China Burma India) forces had bellied up to the bar. When they spotted us at the door they immediately yelled at us to come in for a drink and everyone wanted to buy us a drink including some good looking nurses, all of whom had high ranking bars on their uniforms, like Majors and Lt. Colonels. I hesitated as we were on duty but the MP said, "Why not it was close to the end of our shift," so I succumbed to the offers. I got into a long conversation with a very good looking nurse who was a Major and she wanted to know what ship I was on so I told her, since the war was over I didn't think it was improper to tell her now. She brightened up and said, "That is the ship I'm going back on, I hope I see you on board," I said, "Yes you probably will," knowing that she was going to be off limits to me. We soon finished our shore patrol duty and I returned to the ship.

The next morning I found out that we were going to have a soft ball game that day, so I volunteered to play. Basically the teams were made up from which ever rating you had, for instance the left arm ratings against the right arm ratings. It was kind of a holiday outing and they brought a few cases of beer to the field to quench everyone's thirst. It was greatly appreciated, since it was a hot and muggy day. The first thing we had to do was clear the field of the cows that were munching on the grass. This was a little bit scary because while we were running them off the field a street car came by on the outskirts of the field loaded down with Hindu passengers who looked as if they didn't approve of our running the sacred cows around. However the street car didn't stop in this area so we all breathed a sigh of relief and started to play ball. The game was fun and every one had a chance to play. I think we won by one run as the pitching was pretty poor. I pitched one inning and I think the other side got several singles and a home run, much to my dismay. We had a bottle of Pabst Blue Ribbon or a Coke and returned to the ship feeling good, not from drink but from being able to play at our national past time, baseball.

During both of these trips to Calcutta I always heard crew members talking about buying star sapphires at reasonable prices. Wondering how you knew if you got a real one or a fake one was always brought up in the discussion. Everyone agreed that you should get any gems appraised. Then I brought up the question, could you trust the appraiser? There was a lot of discussion on this point, I decided not to fool around with buying any precious gems, even if I could sell them to Tiffany's in New York, for a big profit. The one thing that I wanted was a pair of hand made walking boots. They ran about 40 dollars in US currency or about 120 rupee's in Indian money. So I figured that I would go to the PX on board ship and buy a few cartons of cigarettes's to use as barter. Why I bought Old Gold cigarettes's I'll never understand but I thought no one on the ship smoked this brand and it would be easier to sneak them ashore rather than any of the more popular brands. On my next liberty I put my bathing suit and five cartons of cigarettes in the bottom of my carrying bag then put a heavy towel on top of everything so that my cigarette cartons wouldn't show. Checking out for liberty at the gangway I unzipped the bag and flashed what was in the bag quickly, saying to the OD, "I'm going swimming down town at the hotel, I sort of mumbled it and the OD didn't pay much attention to what was in the bag so I hurried off the ship and hailed a taxi for town. The first place I went to was the Bank of India. I walked in and went to the information desk and asked to see the manager of the bank. He came out of his office and inquired as to what I wanted. So I asked him if he was interested in any cigarette's. He said yes, so I showed him the five cartons and he said how much and I said I need 120 rupee's for all five cartons. He smiled and said OK, so the deal was made and I walked out of the bank with enough money for my black shiny boots. At the boot shop I found a pair that were just about the right size. I haggled with the clerk and got the price down to about 110 rupee's and we both agreed on the deal so I walked out with a pair of calf high walking boots. These boots had just about the same look as my GI shoes so I could wear them on liberty any time.

Since the war was finally over I thought maybe I should buy something made in Calcutta that would remind me of when I had duty here. Looking around I found a water pipe with a long hose looking attachment made out of fabric with a wooden mouth piece to suck the smoke through the water filled brass holder, the only thing wrong with this instrument was it didn't have a bowl for the tobacco. So off I went looking for a proper bowl to fit on the fancy long tubular holder that sat on top of the water holder. Along the way a young man, well dressed, with a very tan completion who stood about five feet four inches tall, began a conversation with me. I wondered why he wanted to talk to me. Well I found out soon enough. It seemed that he was a scout for the US Army and had just been released from his duties. He told me that he was Burmese and that was the territory where he worked with the Army. I really didn't believe him but he seemed harmless so I let him tag along with me to find a bowl for my water pipe. He suggested that we go to the New Hog Market place to look for it. We entered the huge market place and wandered around looking at all the things that were for sale. There were fancy carpets, cooking bowls, baskets, vegetables, fruit, birds, and jewelry, everything imaginable was in this very large market place. To me the building looked like a great big cow barn. We didn't see any bowls that we could buy. One dealer wanted to sell me a whole set but I was stubborn and thought I could find some one who would sell me the bowl separate. My little Burmese friend said that there were native shops out behind the building in alley way. So we stepped out into the alley and saw that there were plenty of little stalls with merchandise in them like hand made baskets, pottery and stuff that the natives could make and sell for a reasonable price. Looking around I became aware of a large crowd of natives looking at us as if we shouldn't be there. They started towards us just as I found a pottery place where they did have the type of bowl that I wanted. My Burmese escort looked worried as I was haggling over the price of the bowl and told me we had better get out of this area. I looked around and sure enough the crowd was starting to gather around us and looked very menacing. I quickly settled for a higher price than I wanted to and we walked quickly back to the Hog Market back door while the crowd kept looking at us with a definite scowl on everyone's face. My heart was hammering pretty loudly, I thought if they decided to attack us we wouldn't stand a chance as there were no other caucasians around. I was the only one. We stepped into the market place and found more friendly faces to my relief. I thanked the Burmese fellow for helping me and gave him some rupees and told him I was going back to the ship. Before I left him we did discuss the possibility of buying precious stones from Burma which he claimed he could provide but that is as far as that discussion went, it was time to go back to the ship so I started looking for a taxi. I ran into two other members of the crew who were going back, so we got together and caught a cab that would take us back to the basin where the ship was located. I noticed that the driver didn't start his meter as it sat on 00.00. The driver mumbled something about a flat fee for the three of us and we said OK. This was another one of those old touring cars with no top so we got a lot of fresh air. On the way back a passing auto splashed water from a deep puddle and it hit me right in the face. We were sitting in the back seat. I thought ugh!! All those horrible diseases I could get from that dirty water, all I could think of at the time was to try and spit out any liquid in my mouth, anything to keep those germs out of reach. I could hardly wait to get to my locker to gargle in some listerien to get rid of any germs or what ever. When we got to the entrance at the basin the driver informed us that the bill was going to be 25 rupees. We all said baloney and we each tossed him 3 rupees. He complained to the MP at the entrance, so the MP came over and asked him how much was on the meter? That did it, he told the driver to get out of here or he would arrest him for chiseling. We ducked into the yard and the MP said, "Those guys try that on everyone, you guys should watch out for those kinds of tricks."

We loaded up with the returning troops. There were many soldiers with Indian brides, much to my surprise. We also had a large group of Chinese Army soldiers, about 500 of them I believe. We were told that they were going to be going to school in the USA, they were from General Chaing Kai-Shek's Army. Among the Army troops were a group called Merrill's Marauder's, a tough group of fighter's who had made a name for themselves in China and Burma. (According to them the Chinese fighters were lousy and lazy and didn't really do any fighting.) They were very suspicions of the Chinese and told us that they thought they really were communist spies and that they were infiltrating the USA. We started down the river and soon hit the open sea on the Bay of Bengal. When we hit the Indian Ocean we soon discovered that our food supply was a bit short, so we put in a call at an old British Naval Base in Trincomilee, Ceylon. There I saw the French Cruiser Richelieu and the old battle ship King George V. The French cruiser looked sleek but the old battle ship looked as if it should have been retired before World War one. It even had a pointed bow at water level that looked like a big spear which appeared to be a ramming device. There was a British supply ship in the harbor so we negotiated with her for some fresh supplies which she assured us she had. We took on a huge supply of lamb and fresh lettuce, so we thought. We spent the night in this beautiful harbor and watched a full moon come up over the horizon, it was a large orange full moon and looked as big as a house, it was as spectacular as you can view any place in the world, I'll always remember that scene. Walking around the ship I noticed that we had a group of quarters screened off so that those inside could not get out onto the regular deck, in other words they were confined to their quarters. I found out that these were Section Eights, (crazies) and they had all kinds of problems. Looking at them I saw that they were all very pale and thin. The nurse who said she would be on the ship, looked me up and found out where my quarters were. She wanted to come back there and visit me but I didn't encourage her. However she did try get back there but we had marine guards at both the port and starboard entrances to our quarters and I told them not to let any of those Army Nurses into our area. After being rebuffed I never saw that nurse again. We left Trincomalee and headed for Aden and the Red Sea. Much to my amazement I saw some of the crew throwing huge quantities of lettuce and meat over the side. Inquiring as to what was the matter I was told that the health officer declared all those supplies we took on from the British were unfit to eat and he ordered them thrown over the side. On our ship the troops had the same food as we did. They ate in the same mess deck but had a different chow line from ours. I noticed that our food was a little bit different from normal such as canned turkey meat which was served with rice, it was very good. A dish of peaches, that came from some canned food company that tasted almost like fresh peaches. All in all the food seemed to be better than usual.

While in the Indian Ocean the six of us in our nice new quarters became very bored with our time off. We got to comparing our duties and what resources we had that we could use to create some excitement. The gunners mate said laughingly, that they had a surplus of alcohol in 5 gallon tins that was used for the recoil system on the 5 inch 38 cannons. The pharmacist mate said, "I've got silex glass pots and rubber corks for cooking anything." Jack of the dust said, "I can get us pineapple juice anytime. The store keeper said, "I'm in charge of the ice machine" and I said, "Perfect I can get plenty of copper tubing, lets distill some alky." We had a electric hot plate that we used for coffee so we had everything to get us in trouble. We designed a simple distillery by coiling the copper tubing and running it through a tub of ice. As the alky heated up and began to steam it went through the copper tube and dripped into another coffee pot, all the while we made sure that only steam made it through the system. When I came off watch that evening the gang said, "We have a pot of pure 180 proof alcohol, lets test it with some pineapple juice." It was so successful that we invited the chiefs over to help us drink our tropical cocktail. Everyone thought it was delicious and the whole group began to feel very happy! Needless to say, the whole group on the stern quarters had terrific headaches the next morning. Going over to the starboard side into the chiefs quarters to see how they all felt I saw that they were shifting bunks around so I inquired as to what was going on? One of the chiefs growled · that the chief in the top bunk thought he was the fountain of youth during the night and sprinkled everyone below him so they made him shift to the bottom bunk to keep everyone happy. I went back and told my group and we all had a good laugh over that story. During the morning we heard that the Chaplain was searching the ship for a distillery, as he heard that some of the crew had been drinking and he was going to find out where this operation was located. We immediately heaved all the equipment over the side erasing all evidence of that distillery. Of course we saved the silex pots and the rubber corks that fit the pots as this was normal equipment for making coffee and the rubber corks were the pharmacist mates equipment. The chaplain never found out who made the joy juice and after about three days he gave up on his investigation. So, we built another and had another party while going through the Red Sea. Again you could see the wind blowing the sand out over the water in the evening, it was an awesome sight to see. We were told by some one, that the wind on the Sahara Desert could dry your body out in a few hours in that strong wind, and I believed him.

We were going at a pretty good clip, I was told around 21 knots when there was a man over board alarm sound by a look out who spotted the man falling into the sea. The skipper was on the bridge and he quickly started to maneuver the ship into a big turn once we cleared the person in the water. There were several other ships in our area so we ran up signal flags that said we had a man over board, all the ships acknowledged and stood by while we circled around in a very long turn which seemed about a mile in circumference. It took us several minutes to get back to the guy in the water. I was out on deck and spotted him as the skipper piloted the ship as close as possible to him. When we got about a 100 feet away from him and he was about at the midship point I could see that he was swimming with army fatigues and GI boots on. The skipper stood out on the wing of the bridge and yelled through a megaphone, "Son we are going to throw a life ring to you grab it and we will pick you up as soon as possible," All the while I could see he was swimming away from us, he stopped for a second to answer the skipper, took a deep breath and yelled "FU" to the skipper! I almost fell through the deck when I heard his answer. I thought this guy is going to be in deep trouble, the skippers face turned red and yelled at the boat crew to lower the motor launch and go after this guy. Believe it or not they had to chase him with the motor whale boat and grab him by his clothes in order to haul him in the motor launch. By then they knew they had a Section Eight patient so they had to make sure he didn't try and get away from them. That is when we found out that he had broken out of that cage of wire

I saw on the stern of the ship where all those pale faced soldiers were living.

We had smooth sailing through the Mediterranean Sea. As we passed by the Rock of Gibraltar I took a long look at the Rock thinking I probably would never see it again. As we entered the Atlantic Ocean we began to pick up the Fox sked from NSS, the East Coast Naval transmitting station. Now that the war was finally over for sure, we began to get messages about how personnel were going to be discharged. The first thing we copied was a message that there was going to be a point system in order to get a discharge. On the point system, if you were married you got so many points, then there was your time in the service, your time spent overseas, each one of the categories was given a certain number of points with certain restrictions. If you had over fifty points you were able to go for a discharge immediately. The certain restrictions put on essential ratings, these ratings were frozen until such time it was feasible to allow them to apply for their discharge. Wouldn't you know that Radiomen was one of the frozen ratings. Everyone one on the ship started adding up their points. The lowest points held on the ship was a Pvt in the Marines who had come aboard the ship directly from boot camp, he had less than 5 points, everyone kidded him about that. Being in the single category I still had plenty of points to my credit for a discharge when it became possible, I had one hundred and forty five points, almost enough for three guys to get out if it was split among them. It didn't bother me too much as I had nothing on the out side to go to yet. I had always given everybody the impression that I was going stay in the Coast Guard until retirement, because I knew that you were treated differently if they thought you were a twenty year man. As we progressed further into the Atlantic everyone was preparing their belongings for the eventful day of getting off the ship and obtaining their discharge. I even began polishing my boots for liberty in New York City.

Chapter 53.

New York-New York!

We had smooth sailing all the way to New York. When we arrived we hung a big sign on the side of the ship that we had Merrills Marauders on board. It was sure nice to get back to the Big Apple. After unloading the troops we had orders to unload most of the ammo we had on board. I was put in charge of the barge that we were loading on the second day. I saw that they had unloaded around 2000 rounds of ant-aircraft 5 inch 38 shells and quite a few flats of 20 mm shells. This day we were unloading 40 mm shells which were piled on regular flats in their cases. The ammo barge had a roof with an opening on the side of the roof so that the crane operator could swing the flat over the barge's roof . and drop it on the deck, then we would move them into the inside the barge and carefully balance the load as we progressed. Every thing went well until the crane operator misjudged one of his drops and caught the top edge of the opening and spilled the whole flat of 40 millimeters shells all over the deck. With out thinking too much of what might happen I pushed the whole works over the side before anything could explode, or so I thought. I called the OD and told him what happened and he stopped the operation immediately and called the Navy to explain that we had dumped a flat of 40 mm shells into the Hudson river. The Navy immediately sent a diving crew over to retrieve the cases of 40's. We got the rest of the day off and I didn't have to do that job anymore. I had liberty that afternoon so I took off for town, I had to walk through a poor neighbor hood that was adjacent to the harbor on the Hudson river. It was quite a scene as most of the apartments and flats were cold water type flats and there was laundry hanging out of many windows and there seem to be lots of trash on the streets. I think the district was called the Bowery. I finally got to a subway station and took the underground to Times Square. Since it was close to dinner time I spotted Child's Restaurant which seemed like a familiar name to me so I went in to grab a bite to eat. The place was crowded and there wasn't a seat to be had. There was a whole section of the diner roped off that said it couldn't be used. A nice waitress came over and said what can I do for you and I said I would like to have dinner if it was possible. She asked me where I came from, out of curiosity, and I told her I just got back from India, with that she said, I'm not going to let you stand around waiting for a table come with me. She lifted the rope blocking off the empty tables and said here is where you can sit and I will see that you get dinner. These civilians and the boss can't complain about you having a privileged seat in this restaurant It sure made me feel good that some one thought that we deserved a little attention. I had a good meal and left well satisfied with what I had. I came back to the ship around ten PM. There was a lot of commotion going on near the gangway. I could see a seaman talking rapidly to the OD on deck and wondered what was going on. When I got to the quarter deck I found out that this seaman, (a real red neck) from Georgia, had swum across the river from the adjacent pier across from us in the very cold Hudson River. He was telling the OD that his buddy was still in the river! This guy was pretty strong, he was the guy who fought in the ring on the very first trip we took. He and his buddy had jumped ship and gone AWOL for a good time and figured that they could swim back to the ship and climb up the mooring lines and sneak on board with out being caught. The up shot of this was his buddy couldn't make it across the cold water to the ship and had given up. This guy didn't help him so it was assumed that he had drowned. The OD sent out the alarm that some one was in the river and had apparently didn't make it out of the drink. The harbor patrol dragged the river and sure enough they retrieved the body. The sad part of this story is that his mother would not receive life insurance policy the government had on him because he had jumped ship and was AWOL, which also meant he would have gotten a Bad Conduct Discharge if he had lived. The Georgia Cracker got life imprisonment for his part in the action, so I was told later on. This all happened at a very inopportune time for them as it was in the coldest part of country, you could see small bits of ice floating on the surface of the river at night. The month was October and you could feel the rapid change in the weather. I remember how one day it was a nice warm day and then the next day it turned real cold which surprised me very much as I, being from California was not used to this kind of change. Another thing that I witnessed was St. Elmo's fire on the rigging of the ship while we were in port. It was the weirdest thing I have ever seen, there were little streaks of lightening hitting the ships guy wires and antennae, I was a bit leery of this phenomenon but was quite fascinated by it. The next night my friend Chief Warrant Williams wanted to go on liberty with me so off we went down town. To hit all the bars on Times Square. We got to one very large bar and decided to have something to eat. They served food at the bar so I ordered some spaghetti and meat balls, and my friend Officer Williams ordered the same thing. We ordered a glass of wine with our dinner and I started to eat mine. It was a good meal but half way through the meal I heard Officer Williams exclaim "Swede look at me", I glanced over at saw that he had let his upper false teeth drop down on his lowers and he was shoveling the spaghetti through the top part of his mouth. I started laughing so hard I couldn't eat the rest of my meal. The bartender looked at him aghast and picked up a phone to tell some one about what he was seeing. It wasn't too long when two shore patrol sailors came in and told us that we would have to go back to the ship. So we rode back to the ship and they escorted Chief Warrant Officer Paul Williams up to the OD on the quarter deck and said he was confined to the ship until he sobered up. I was told that I could go back down town if I wanted to, as I hadn't been acting up. I went back down town but didn't stay long as it wasn't much fun roaming around Times Square alone.

Rebel our chief radioman told me that we were going to be going back to Calcutta again in a few days but he was trying to get us West Coast crew members transferred back to Oakland or San Francisco before the ship left. He had a pretty good in with the skipper as they were together on an AK cargo ship that was sunk in the South Pacific in the early part of the war. He said the skipper was trying to get a hold of his good friend the Under Secretary of the Navy but he was having trouble with the phone lines as there was some kind of a long distance operators strike going on but he would keep trying. We all hoped he would be able to get through to the Secretary before we started out for Calcutta again. It is now the day we will sail and no word as yet about our status on that transfer! At ten o'clock in the morning Rebel came into the shack and said "Swede and all you West Coast guys get ready to leave the ship your papers are all made out for all five of you and Swede will be in charge of the group while you are in transit. Boy did we get our things together in a hurry, we saw the chief yeoman and got our orders to catch the New York Central for Chicago and head for the Bay Area. We boarded the train and found out that we had Pullman class tickets as the Coast Guard under the Treasury Department always traveled first class.

Chapter 54.

Transcontinental.

The New York Central tracks go up through Canada via the city of Windsor then on to Chicago. I think we passed through Detroit also, I got to thinking that the World Series was going to be played in Detroit this week end with a National league team, I thought it would be neat to see a game but we couldn't adjust our schedule for any thing like that. In the morning we all trooped up to the dining car and sat down to have breakfast. We all took a good look at the menu and decided what

499

we wanted when the waiter came in with a few plates of scrambled eggs and set them down at our table. I looked up at him and said, "What is this all about I didn't order scrambled eggs," he said, "That's what you get when you're on military script coupons. My reply was take this stuff away we didn't order this food. I told him to bring me bacon and eggs sunny side with brown toast and coffee. He started arguing with me. I said, "Please have the Captain of the Military Police come in here to settle this right now." In the meantime my charges were very silent wondering what was going to happen. The waiter chickened out and took away the scrambled egg dishes and came back and took our orders. You see the script was for three dollars and fifty cents worth of breakfast and what he brought was worth about one dollar and ninety five cents. I knew exactly what this was all about, they were making about two dollars on every GI that ate a meal with that military script. We watched him very carefully to make sure he didn't pull a fast one, We let the manager of the dinning car know that we knew what was going on and if we didn't get our fair return for coupons we were going to complain to the Military Police who were riding on the train to safe guard all passengers. We had no more trouble from the porters or waiters after that and we soon entered Chicago. Here we had to travel by bus to the Southern Pacific train at the West side (I think) train station for the rest of the trip to Oakland. We had a short wait before boarding the Southern Pacific train to the West Coast but not enough time to look over Chicago so we all decided to look for a bar. We found one near by and proceeded to have a few beers. We soon boarded the train and found our Pullman seats for the long ride to Oakland. The train started out on time and we were on our way. We found out that the engine was a coal burner and it was throwing out a lot of black soot which penetrated the windows and soon we all felt gritty. Nobody cared because we were on our way home. Looking out of the window at the scenery I discovered that when we crossed the Mississippi river it was a yellow brown color not the clear water as I always imagined. I'm not sure if it was the old Mississippi, it could have been the Missouri any way I was disappointed that the color was so muddy looking. We were having a great time exchanging story's with all the other G I's on the train. There were a lot of good looking WAC'S on board also. We soon became acquainted with them and had a lot of fun. When we were getting near Ogden, Utah, we stopped some place in Wyoming and every one said this is where you can get a great big juicy T bone steak. I saw a bar along side the tracks about a hundred feet away and told everyone that I would jump off the train to buy a few beers. I ran as fast as

I could into the bar and asked if I could buy a few quarts of beer? The bar tender quickly came up with four quarts of beer which I paid for and held them close to my chest so that I could run if the train started to move. As I left the bar the train began to start out so I ran as fast as I could holding the beers tightly. One of the guys was hanging out on the stairs of the car so I passed him the bottles of beer while running along side the train, it was still moving slowly but picking up speed. I handed all of the bottles to the guy on the first step and grabbed the hand rail to steady my self all the time thinking that I was glad I hadn't missed the train. How would I explain that one to the Coast Guard if I had not been able to get on board? We carried the beer back to our seat and sat down to have a cool one. Since it was near bed time we pulled the curtains closed so that we had some privacy in the lower section and arranged the seats so that they were facing each other. There were three of us and three WAC'S. About that time in came the MP's and they jerked open the curtains and looked in. I thought, "oh oh here we go in trouble," but all they said was, "Don't get rowdy and make a lot of noise, if you can do that we won't bother you," we said, "OK we will be careful." We had a lot of fun singing and telling stories and drinking beer, we used the paper cups from the trains drinking fountain. The next morning we had a chance to view the Salt Lake as we traveled across it. It looked like snow it was so white. When we pulled into Reno we all jumped out and played a few nickels in the slot machines at the station. Of course, no one won anything but it was kind of fun. One of my guys told me that he came from Auburn, Callifornia and he was wondering if he could maybe get off there and then make it into San Francisco on his own. So we set up a plan, the day we arrived in

San Francisco was a Friday so I told everyone if they could all make it to the Ferry Building on Monday morning we could all go home and meet there on Monday and go to the district office together. They all said that they could do it so I said if anyone is missing we will be in big trouble they all assured me that they would be there at 10 o'clock Monday morning, so I said, "OK lets do it." When we got to Auburn our first traveler got off and we all bid him good bye, saying, "We'll see you Monday morning." The rest of us all parted in Oakland and we said our good byes and planned to see each other next week. My folks met me at the Ferry Building in the car so I went home feeling great but dirty from that long five day trip. The next Monday morning I nervously stood around the Ferry building waiting for all the guys to show up. Sure enough every one showed up and we all hiked over to the District Office and reported in. The first class yeoman took the papers I had carried and looked them over when he exclaimed, "It took you guys a whole year to get here?" I said, "Huh! There must be some mistake," then he says, "Oh I see that dumb yeoman back east made a mistake on that first date all the rest are for this year not last year 1944." He said, "Seven days to get here sounds reasonable." You're all going over to Government Island and wait for assignments or discharges. I was given liberty every night so I would go home to enjoy the company of my family. I soon was transferred to the receiving station at Bay and Powell for my discharge. On November 2 1945 I was interviewed by a Lt Jg Spar and asked if I would like to ship over as a permanent chief radioman. I still had pictures in my mind of those old pot bellied chiefs I had been working with for six years and 5 days and thought about all the lousy duties and bad chow I had encountered while in the service and the fact that they had control of you to do what ever they wanted you to do, so I told her, "No I want out." She said, "You still have thirty days to make up you mind, also they will give you a rating of permanent chief radioman," I said, "Thank you I'll think about it." I didn't check my discharge papers as I should have, because there was no mention of me being stationed at Diamond Head Radio station NMO. Apparently it was on my service records as I had no trouble getting my Pearl Harbor Medallion when I applied for it later on in the 1990's. Just as I was getting my discharge I ran into one of my co workers that had been on my watch at NMC. S.F Radio. His name was Jocko LaRoach and he was a real Jockey who had joined the Coast Guard and held a rating of second class radioman. Since we were both getting out at the same time we decided to go out of the receiving station and cross over the street to a little bar and have a last drink while we were still officially in the C.G. We had our drink and discussed the possibility of burning our uniform out in the street in celebration of getting out of the of the service. Since we didn't have any other clothes we thought this would be a bad deal. He told me he had gotten married to his long time girl friend and that he had promised her he would take her to the movies that night. He said, "Since you know Mary why don't you go with us, its supposed to be a good movie and its one of the neighbor hood movie houses." I had nothing pending so I went with them for a last fling and saw a pretty good movie. I went home after the picture and had dinner with my folks. I felt pretty good about the way I won the war on this day November 2nd, nineteen forty five. Which took me six years, seven days and twelve hours to accomplish.

The next morning I had to go to the draft board in down town Mill Valley. I decided not to mention that threatening draft notice to me in 1941, when they were getting real serious about drafting all of us poor souls. I had my discharge with me and all they did was give me a card saying that my draft status was 1C which meant that I was not draftable. It was then that I realized they were still drafting, they hadn't formally declared that the war was over. They told me to carry that card with me just like my driver's license. I couldn't believe that I came out of this conflict with only a bloody nose, on the Edge of War, so to speak! My final act was to go to the county court house and register my discharge papers with the county recorder.

George C. Larsen

Here are some other titles for this story.

Adventures of a Coast Guard sailor in World War 11.

What Coast are you Guarding?

Some adventures of the step child navy during WW2

How Some Of Us Fought World War Two!

A Coast Guard sailors view of ww2

How I won WW2!

How I survived in the Coast Guard after Dec -7, 1941.

George C. Larsen

What's a Shallow Water sailor doing in the Indian
    Ocean?

What's the Hooligan Navy doing here?

How the enlisted man felt in the Coast Guard.

How this swabbie felt about the War!

No shot fired in anger.

Addendum to my ON the Edge of War story.

After spending some time wondering what to do about work. I first tried going into business with my brother-inlaw. We both bought surplus dump trucks and I bought a front end loader tractor. We had a good idea but couldn't get enough work to pay off our loans so I gave up and went to work as an operating engineer, taking care of heavy equipment like bull-dozers and cranes. The pay was pretty good, so I got rid of the loans and found enough money to buy a 1941 Ford convertible from a dealer in my home town, Mill Valley.

Six months after getting out of the U.S. Coast Guard, I got a call from my shipmate Rebel Allen, my former Chief Radioman. He told me he was calling from his aunts house in San Anselmo, California, which is about ten miles from where I was living. He said he looked up my folks phone number and called just in case I was around. He invited me to come up and visit that day, as it would be the only time for awhile that he and the family would be at the aunt's place. So, I dashed up there in my new convertible and was greeted by him and his wife with great delight. He then introduced me to his sister-inlaw, who happened to be with her sister to help her as she was pregnant with her second child. Well, to make a long story short, we got along so well that we got engaged to be married after the birth of her sister's child on November 2,

1946, exactly one year to the day when I was discharged from the service.

My bride was an ex WAC, who was a cover girl for the Army (News Week magazine, the December 25th 1945 issue) and she modeled most of their uniforms for various magazines during her time in the Army, she also did recruiting for the WAC'S. We spent some time in Jenner-By-The-Sea while I worked for a contractor. We worked for the California Highway Department on Highway One, the coastal road along the California Coast. As Christmasn season came up we decided that this wasn't for me, so I quit and we moved to her home town Portland, Oregon where I found a job with Northwest Pacific Bell, stringing new lines in rural areas of Oregon. After six months of working in the freezing weather of the North West, I decided to go back to school under the GI Bill. Patricia thought she could get a job while I was going to school, which turned out to be the best thing going for us. I signed up at Multnomah College in their Technical classes. With my back ground in radio this was just ticket for me. The school program was a five day week and about six hours of classes each day, dealing with Math, Electrical Engineering, Shop Technic, such as building and designing electronic circuits, broadcasting in radio and television stations and many other electronic devices. Before I gaduated I obtained an Amateur General Class License and a First Class Radio Telephone License. After I graduated in the spring of 1949 I was offered a job by letter from the Bureau of Roads, a government agency, just because of my schooling offering me a job on their survey group as a S-3 Engineer, just because of my schooling! This was quite a surprise, since I didn't solicit for this job. It was a new experience for me, as I worked with the foreman laying out super's on curves in the road, using my math that was hammered into my head at school. After about three months of work I got a letter from one of my school chums saying that there was an opening in radio in the town of Missoula, Montana and I could get the job if I wanted it. So, I did an interview at their Portland station and was hired. The pay wasn't great but I wanted the experience, so up to Missoula I went, leaving my wife in Portland, since she had a good job and I could come home on week ends. I lasted about six months doing that, when I got a letter form one of my sisters that RCA was hiring technicians in San Francisco for Television installations. The pay in Missoula wasn't that good so I decided to try for a job there. Being a native of that area, it was a good chance to become familiar with this new media and be around the family. My wife, Patricia, got a transfer to San Francisco with her same company and we rented an apartment in San Francisco, where we lived and worked for two and a half years. Television finally came to Portland, Oregon, so RCA moved a bunch of us up to Portland, to prepare for the opening of the first commercial UHF Station, KPTV. Particia was extremely happy to move back to her home town. By now we had a baby girl and wanted to buy a house to raise our family properly. We found a new bungalow for just the right price. After about six months I got a call from a school chum who was working at KPTV, saying that they needed 2 technicians.

After talking to the Chief Engineer about salary, I informed RCA that I was going to take a job with KPTV. That started me on a long career as a TV Engineer in Portland and San Francisco, doing studio and news camera work to Lighting Director and Studio Supervisor. I retired in 1985 around June first and found time to write my memoirs. I want to thank all of those people who encouraged me to keep going on this story and I hope they all buy a copy!

They are, Margeret Anglade, Jackie my Librarian, Frank Myles, Ernie Furst, Alice Sherry, Peggy Malliet. Last but Least, my Editor Sheila Berg and Tracy & David Brooks. Thank you all- GEORGE C. LARSEN

Printed in the United States
1500300002B/31-279